CIRCUIT HIKES

in

SHENANDOAH
NATIONAL
PARK

Potomac Appalachian Trail Club
2013
Reprinted in 2015

Circuit Hikes in Shenandoah National Park

17th Edition (2013)

Text by
Michael Barreda

Editing by
John Hedrick

Photos by
Larry Broadwell, Lee Sheaffer, John Hedrick

Maps by
Dave Pierce

Library of Congress Cataloging-in-Publication Data

Barreda, Michael.
Circuit hikes in Shenandoah National Park / text by Michael
Barreda ; editing by John Hedrick ; photos by Larry Broadwell;
maps by Dave Pierce. -- 17th ed.
p. cm.
ISBN 978-0-915746-67-5
1. Hiking--Virginia--Shenandoah National Park--Guidebooks.
2. Shenandoah National Park (Va.)--Guidebooks. I. Title.
GV199.42.V82S483 2013
917.55'9044--dc23
2012031861

Cover photo: Dark Hollow Falls, photo by Lee Sheaffer
Inside front cover: Upper cascade in Doyles River, photo by Lee Sheaffer

Table of Contents

Introduction

North District

Central District

South District

ACKNOWLEDGEMENTS

PATC thanks the following for their efforts to update and ensure the accuracy of this book:

Melissa Rudacille and John Buchheit of the National Park Service;

PATC volunteers Mel Ellis, Melanie Perl, Noel Freeman, Elizabeth Freeman, Casey Buboltz, Cindy Ardecki, Elizabeth Rood, John Hedrick, Dave Pierce, Megan McCune and Shirley Schulz

And a Special Salute to the PATC trail building, maintenance and patrol crews
North, Central and South Districts
of Shenandoah National Park

Without their work, this book and countless hours of delight in our park would not have been possible.

POTOMAC APPALACHIAN TRAIL CLUB (PATC)

118 Park St. S.E., Vienna, VA 22180

703.242.0315; www.patc.net

This guide is published by Potomac Appalachian Trail Club (PATC, a volunteer group whose main purpose is preservation and maintenance of part of the Appalachian Trail (AT) and other trails in the mid-Atlantic region. We provide a variety of guides, maps and other publications. We offer hiking, climbing, and ski-touring excursions, as well as opportunities for training and volunteer service. Our office is open Mon-Fri, 11:30am-1:30pm except holidays. Visitors and callers are welcome.

Changes in trails occur occasionally and make it difficult to keep any guide current. Please report any errors or changes you find to "Editor - PATC" at the above address to enhance future editions. PATC expressly denies any liability for any accident or injury to persons using trails described in its publications.

LEAVE NO TRACE

With so many people enjoying parks and wilderness areas, good trail ethics are essential. Please leave these places the same or in better condition than you found them. Do not pick wildflowers or bother wildlife. Pack out all you bring in (including toilet paper), and any litter that you find. Camp at the park-prescribed distance from any water source to avoid contaminating it. Use a camp stove instead of building a fire. Wear camp shoes to minimize damage to vegetation and avoid camping in meadows. **It is a federal offense to remove or alter artifacts at cultural resource sites such as homesteads or cemeteries.**

INTRODUCTION

This book describes 29 areas that offer circuit hikes (routes that require little if any walking over the same ground more than once). In all, 40 circuits are described. They are listed in geographical order from north to south along Skyline Drive. Some circuits are relatively flat, while others are rugged rock scrambles; some are short strolls, while others are all-day, exhausting trips. Determine how many miles or how much time you want to spend on a hike, then read the descriptions to find the hike that suits you and your companions.

TIPS AND TERMINOLOGY

Circuit Lengths are rounded to the nearest 0.1 mile. Distances were measured shortly before publication, and may not agree with distances posted on trail signs. Over time, trail relocations to limit erosion and other changes occur, changing routes and distances.

Time Estimates are based on a hiking speed of 2 miles/hr plus 30 minutes for each 1,000ft gain in elevation. Some estimates are longer, to adjust for ruggedness and steepness of the terrain.

Difficulty Ratings are based on ruggedness of trail, elevation change during the hike, and overall distance traveled. This guide uses three ratings: easy, moderate and strenuous.

Elevation Change Estimates indicate the sum of the ascents on a circuit, not just the difference between the highest and lowest points of the circuit.

Maps are drawn to 100 ft contour intervals. For more complete maps of the Park, refer to PATC Map #9 (North District), #10 (Central District), and #11 (South District) and PATC Shenandoah map app in iphone or android format. Shows full content of Maps 9, 10, 11 with GPS tracking of your location, even without WiFI or cell reception. Available for $4.99 at Google

Play (requires Android 2.3 or higher) or iTunes App Store (using iOS 4.3 or higher).

Distances on Skyline Drive are marked by mileposts beside the road. This guide uses the mileposts (abbreviated "MP") to locate trailheads.

Trail Signs appear and disappear from time to time, though the Park's use of concrete posts with metal bands limits theft and vandalism. Use maps to keep track. Do not depend strictly on signs.

Park Entrance Fees in 2015: $10 for a 7-day pass from December to February; $15 for a 7 day pass from March to November; $30 for an annual pass. Special rates for senior citizens and others may apply.

Safety— Leave your planned route and target return time with someone who will take action if you go missing. Cell phone reception in the Park is unpredictable at best; do not rely on it. Hike with a friend. Stay on marked trails to avoid getting lost. Do not climb on or around waterfalls. In windy weather, watch for hanging limbs and standing dead trees.

Weather is more extreme in the mountains than at lower elevations, and it can change rapidly. Carry raingear, a sweater, extra food, and plenty of water. Be familiar with symptoms and treatment of both hypothermia and heat-induced problems.

Ticks—After hiking, always check thoroughly for ticks, and watch for signs of tick-borne disease. Lyme disease symptoms may include a red "bullseye" rash at the site of the tick bite, fever, malaise and muscle aches. Without prompt treatment, long-term health can suffer.

Venomous Snakes—Timber rattlesnakes and copperheads may be encountered on any of these hikes. They are not aggressive, but they do not tolerate being approached or stepped on. Be careful placing your feet and hands, especially in rocky areas.

Protective clothing, repellent and sunscreen are recommended. High-top boots, well broken in, and long pants can ward off ankle injuries, blisters, ticks, briars and other problems.

Parking along roads outside the Park and hiking in can get you ticketed or worse. Most circuits in this book use parking areas along Skyline Drive or other authorized trailheads.

Water—Although springs and streams may look clean, the water is unsafe to drink unless filtered, boiled for a full minute, or purified by chemicals (chlorine or iodine). Unless you have such gear, bring your water or get it from a safe source en route to the trailhead.

Camping—Family campgrounds are available for a fee, with a 30-day limit, during the spring, summer and fall. Backcountry camping is allowed, but requires a (free) permit, available at entrance stations, visitor centers and Park headquarters.

Hiking Season—The Park does not close in winter though Skyline Drive may close if road conditions warrant. The circuits change markedly with the seasons. Each season has its own rewards, ranging from winter's unobstructed vistas to the spectacular color in fall, the abundance of wildflowers in spring, and the refreshing summer dips in the Park's many streams.

More Park Information:
On the Web, visit www.nps.gov/shen;
or phone 540-999-3500 for recorded information.

ABBREVIATIONS

AT	Appalachian Trail	yd	yards
ft	feet	mi	miles
hr	hours	MP	Skyline Drive milepost
min	minutes	SR	state road
Mtn	Mountain		
PATC	Potomac Appalachian Trail Club		
SNP	Shenandoah National Park		

LEGEND

Trail Blazes

Single blazes marks the trail

Double blaze means "watch for change in direction"

Roads

MP 20

Primary roads, usually paved
Skyline Drive Milepost

================ Gravel roads or SNP fire roads

Trails

· · · · · · · · · · · · · · · Appalachian Trail (white blaze)

— · — · — · — · — Other trails
    Blue blazes for a foot trail
    Yellow blazes for horse & foot

—·—·— • • • • ===== Set of trails or roads comprising
the described circuit hike

Symbols

Shelter or Hut,   PATC Cabin

Gate,   Spring

— · · — · · — · · — SNP Boundary Line

PARK HISTORY AND GEOLOGY

In 1926, Congress authorized the establishment of Shenandoah National Park. Because no federal funds were allocated, it took ten years for the state of Virginia and contributions from a number of its residents to acquire land for the Park. July of 1931 saw ground-breaking for work on Skyline Drive. President Franklin D. Roosevelt, an ardent supporter, dedicated the Park in a ceremony in July, 1936, and the Drive was completed in 1939. Hundreds of residents were forced out by the Park's creation, through a process that still evokes controversy.

With over 500 miles of hiking and horse trails throughout its 196,000 acres of backcountry spanning an elevation range of 3,500 feet, Shenandoah National Park offers a wide array of activities for every type of visitor. The majority of the Park is on the Blue Ridge Mountains, a part of the Appalachians that is among the oldest in North America, and whose bedrock is primarily granitic and volcanic.

FLORA AND FAUNA

The Park is more than just beautiful scenery. It has over 1,000 flowering plants, 200 bird species, and bigger wildlife including fox, white-tailed deer, and increasingly plentiful black bears.

Spring brings bloodroot, coltsfoot, periwinkle, dogwood, and columbine. Early summer brings out azaleas, golden ragwort, violets, and marsh marigold. The Park bursts into mid-summer with black-eyed susan, Queen Anne's lace, asters, mountain laurel, and evening primrose. Fall colors on the trees are complemented by harebell and goldenrod at ground level.

Over 100 species of trees fill the Park. While the American chestnut once dominated, its numbers have dropped drastically due to chestnut blight. Oak and hickory are now the most common trees, but black locust is often found in fields and meadows, while pitch pine, Virginia pine, and scrub oak are found in the southern section on drier slopes. Cove hardwoods, red oak, ash, and basswood are common along the stream banks. Stately hemlocks that used to line many of the streams have been killed off by an accidental import – Asian insect called the woolly adelgid.

Bear peek-a-boo in the Park, photo by Lee Sheaffer

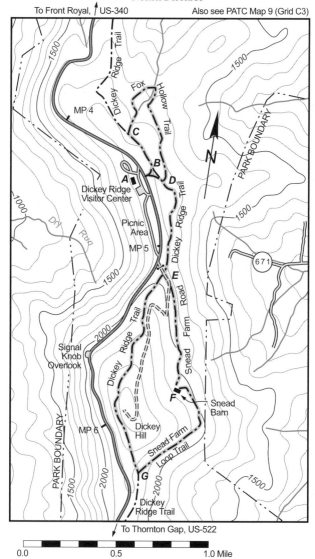

Hike No. 1

FOX FARM—
SNEAD FARM LOOP

1

Length:	5.0 mi
Time Estimate:	3 hr 30 min
Difficulty:	Easy
Elev. Change:	1000 ft

Description: This circuit explores historic remains at the northern end of the Park. Its two separate loops and the nearby amenities of Dickey Ridge Visitor Center offer an easy introduction to the Park. The first loop descends through ruins of the old Fox Farm homestead, where huge rock piles from cleared fields, stone foundations, the Fox cemetery, and old stone walls are visible. The second loop passes Snead barn and a bunkhouse foundation. The circuit also offers panoramic views to the west over Shenandoah Valley from a hang glider launch site. **Pets are not allowed on the Fox Hollow Trail.**

Access: Go to Dickey Ridge Visitor Center, which is 0.4 mi north of MP 5 on Skyline Drive.

Directions:
A **0.0** From flagpole on Drive side of Visitor Center, walk directly across Skyline Drive to Dickey Ridge Trail map and signpost.
B Beyond map and post, take left fork and in 75 yd turn left at concrete signpost onto Dickey Ridge Trail [blue-blazed].
C **0.3** At concrete post, turn right onto Fox Hollow Trail [blue- blazed]. Descend past stone remains of Fox homestead, ascend a little, then descend past Fox cemetery and cross a seasonal wet area. Ascend and turn right onto a steep farm road along a low stone wall. Bear left onto level level tread, then turn right and ascend a short distance.
D **1.3** Turn left at concrete signpost onto Dickey Ridge Trail.

E   **1.8** Turn left at signpost onto Snead Farm Road (blue-blazed), and shortly face two forks in the road. At concrete post marking first fork, take road left, downhill. At concrete post for second fork, bear right, uphill (Powerline crosses the road here, offering a long view east.) Where powerline leaves road bear left and continue on wide, level road.

F   **2.5** Snead Farm Road ends at Snead barn on right, with long stone foundation for house straight ahead. Bear left across grass, as if to skirt the house remains. At concrete post, turn left onto Snead Farm Loop Trail [blue-blazed]. Descend, then turn right onto old farm road.

G   **3.2** Turn right at concrete signpost onto Dickey Ridge Trail and climb. Blue blazes may be sparse here.
3.5 Descend sharply on left fork, which leads 65 yd to overlook with panorama west, where trail passes below hang glider launch site. Browntown is circled by mountains to left; directly west across South Fork of Shenandoah River is Massanutten Mountain, with Great North Mountain beyond Massanutten.
3.6 Reach highest point on trail and begin long descent.

E   **4.3** Turn left onto Snead Farm Road [blue-blazed], then immediately right at signpost to quit road and rejoin blue-blazed Dickey Ridge Trail.

D   **4.9** Turn left at concrete post that marks one end of Fox Hollow Trail, leaving Dickey Ridge Trail to ascend path along edge of grassy field.

A   **5.0** Cross Drive and return to Dickey Ridge Visitor Center.

Hike No. 2

BLUFF TRAIL

2

Length:	13.8 mi
Time Estimate:	8 hr
Difficulty:	Strenuous
Elev. Change:	2100 ft

Description: The circuit starts on the Appalachian Trail, which ascends North Marshall (3368 ft) and South Marshall (3212 ft) on a moderate grade. North Marshall's cliffs and lookout points on South Marshall offer views of surrounding peaks and valleys. Gravel Springs hut is reserved for "long term" back-packers (on trips for 3+ nights) with permits. On the return, Bluff Trail is nearly level and passes through a splendid stand of forest. The final leg on Mount Marshall Trail includes a moderate climb. The side trip to Big Devils Overlook, adding about one mile and an extra 500 ft climb for the round trip, is worthwhile. Late summer weeds may be high on any Park trail, but hiking traffic in this area usually keeps the paths open.

Access: Go to parking area on Skyline Drive between MP 12 and 13. Park about 50 yd north of Jenkins Gap Overlook (2355 ft) on west side of Drive (across from overlook).

Directions:

A 0.0 Find signpost on west side of Drive and follow yellow-blazed trail 180 ft downhill from parking area to AT [white-blazed]. Turn left (south) onto AT and climb.
0.1 Cross old road, ascend through old apple orchard, then descend.
1.7 Cross Drive and climb AT steadily uphill to top of North Marshall, where trail levels. Descend from North Marshall past views to west.
4.0 Cross Drive and climb AT to top of South Marshall and then descend.

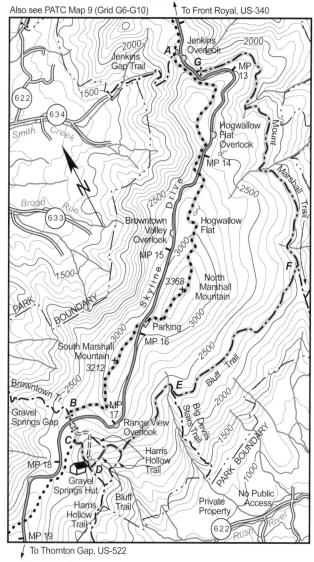

To Thornton Gap, US-522

0.0   0.5   1.0 Mile

16

B **5.6** Pass Browntown Trail [yellow-blazed], which enters on right, and continue on AT. In Gravel Springs Gap (2655 ft), cross Drive to parking area. Avoid yellow-blazed fire road and follow AT downhill.

C **5.8** Turn left at concrete signpost on Gravel Springs Hut trail [blue-blazed] and follow switchbacks down to Gravel Springs. Gravel Springs Hut(reserved for backpackers with permits) is to right of trail.

D **6.0** Turn left at intersection to find Bluff Trail and in 80 ft turn right at signpost, on Bluff Trail [yellow-blazed].
  6.1 Where yellow-blazed Harris Hollow Trail enters on left (trails merge), continue straight, following yellow-blazes.
  6.2 At signpost in left-turning switchback, turn left to continue on Bluff Trail. (Harris Hollow Trail goes straight.)

E **7.5** Continue on yellow-blazed Bluff Trail past Big Devils Stairs Trail [blue-blazed]. (Big Devils Stairs Trail descends 0.5 mi to spectacular view from Big Devils Overlook.)

F **9.9** Turn left at concrete signpost onto Mount Marshall Trail [yellow-blazed].
  10.1 Cross Jordan River (small stream here).
  11.2 Cross Sprucepine Branch.
  12.1 Cross Waterfall Branch.

G **13.4** Turn right (north) along Drive.

A **13.8** Pass Jenkins Gap Overlook and arrive at parking area.

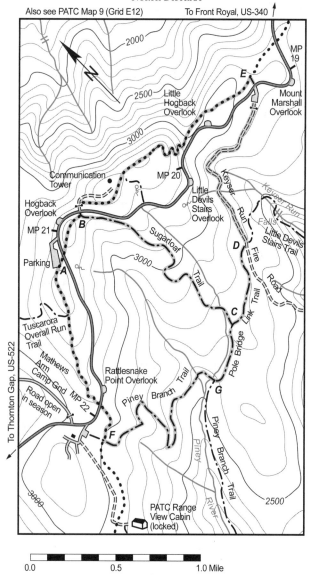

Hike No. 3
SUGARLOAF

3

	Short Circuit	Long Circuit
Length:	5.3 mi	10.1 mi
Time Estimate:	2 hr 45 min	5 hr 30 min
Difficulty:	Easy	Moderate
Elev. Change:	700 ft	1600 ft

Description: The first loop of this figure 8 hike constitutes the short circuit. It descends the eastern slope, then climbs Hogback Mountain's highest peak (3474 ft, with fine views northeast over Browntown Valley to Dickey Ridge and west to Massanutten Mountain), and follows the Appalachian Trail back to the starting point. The second loop descends the east slope again to cross Piney River (not a difficult ford, except in unusually high water), then climbs back to the AT on Sugarloaf Trail. The top of Sugarloaf once more provides great views to the north and east.

Access: The circuit begins on Skyline Drive at a paved parking lot with 10 spaces just south of Hogback Overlook and MP 21, and just north of where the AT crosses the Drive.

Directions:
A **0.0** Find white-blazed AT where it passes a few feet south of parking lot. Angle left across Drive to follow AT north.
B **0.3** Turn right onto Sugarloaf Trail [blue-blazed]. Begin descent through mountain laurel and forest toward Piney River crossing.
C **1.8** Shortly after crossing braided stream, turn left onto Pole Bridge Link Trail [blue-blazed].
D **2.3** At "Fourway" junction, go left on Keyser Run Fire Rd.
E **3.3** Pass gate, cross Drive, and find trail directly across from Keyser Run Fire Road. Walk 200 ft, go left on AT.
 3.7 Climb to top of Little Hogback. Fine view of Massanutten Mtn from ledge 30 ft to right of trail.

3.8 Continue on AT past marked spur trail that leads to Little Hogback Overlook on Drive. Veer right, descend, and then climb steeply via switchbacks up east face of Hogback Mtn to ridge crest. Continue along ridge.

4.5 Pass a few ft left of Hogback's first peak (3420 ft).

4.7 Spur trail leads left, downhill, 0.2 mi to walled-in spring. Continue on AT, beginning to climb. In a few ft, pass hang glider launching area with view of Browntown Valley and Massanutten Mtn.

B **5.0** Turn left onto service road and continue to gate. Cross Drive and pass Sugarloaf Trail turnoff. Continue on AT. Rocky outcrop 15 ft off AT above Hogback Overlook (3440 ft) offers splendid view of Browntown Valley, Dickey Ridge and Massanutten Mtn.

A **5.3** Cross Drive to west of Hogback Overlook. **If hiking only first half of circuit:** stop at parking lot. **For full circuit:** continue on AT. In short distance pass spur trail which leads left 30 ft to 4th peak of Hogback Mt. (3440 ft).

5.7 Pass Tuscarora-Overall Run Trail turnoff on right. Descend past views from outcrop to right.

6.3 Cross Drive and continue on AT.

F **6.6** Turn left onto Piney Branch Trail [blue-blazed]. Descend through old apple orchard and cross Piney River.

G **8.0** Turn left onto Pole Bridge Link Trail [blue-blazed].

C **8.4** Turn left onto Sugarloaf Trail (blue-blazed), cross Piney River, and ascend through mountain laurel.

B **9.8** Turn left (south) onto white-blazed AT, pass above Hogback Overlook once again and continue toward point where AT crosses Drive.

A **10.1** Arrive at parking lot west of Hogback Overlook.

Mountain Laurel

Hike No. 4

PINEY RIDGE—
OVERALL RUN AREA

4

	Little Devils Stairs	Piney Branch	Perimeter Circuit
Length:	7.5 mi	10.1	12.7
Time Estimate:	4 hr 45 min	6 hr 15 min	7 hr 45 min
Difficulty:	Moderate	Strenuous	Strenuous
Elev. Change:	1800 ft	2500 ft	3000 ft
Map Directions:	A-B-C-D-B-A	A-B-E-K-C-D-B-A	A-B-E-F-G-H-I-J-K-C-D-B-A

Description: This area offers many potential circuits. The three covered here all pass the old Bolen cemetery and climb the steep, rocky and scenic Little Devils Stairs on Keyser Run ravine. The ravine's ruggedness and sheer cliffs make it treacherous when wet or icy – better to be climbed than descended, since the probability and consequences of an uphill fall are less. The shortest, the Little Devils Stairs Circuit, descends via Keyser Run Fire Road, then climbs back up the ravine. The Piney Branch Circuit explores another stream valley with two waterfalls before swinging back for the Stairs ascent. The Perimeter Circuit stays close to the Drive on relatively gentle terrain for nearly 4 mi, then descends 1200 ft, passing the Dwyer cemetery (gravesites dating from late 1800s), to Hull School Trail and the Stairs for the return.

Access from Skyline Drive: Go to parking lot for about 10 cars 0.4 mi south of MP 19 at Keyser Run Fire Road. Pass gate on east side of Drive to begin hike. Perimeter Circuit may be shortened 1.6 mi by parking at Piney Ridge lot just south of MP 22, and hiking down to point [**F**] to start the circuit.

Directions for Little Devils Stairs Circuit:
A 0.0 Cross gate (Elev 2900 ft) and begin descent of Keyser

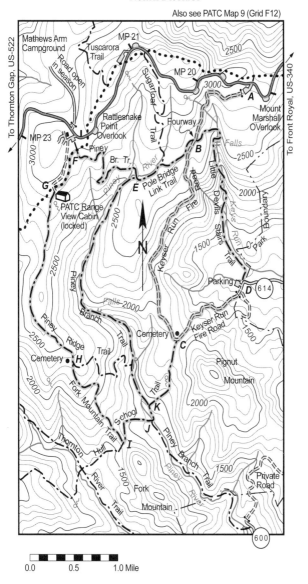

Run Fire Road [yellow-blazed].

B   **1.0** Pass through intersection known as Fourway and continue descending on Keyser Run Fire Road.

C   **3.3** At concrete signpost where Hull School Trail [yellow-blazed] enters from right, swing left to continue down Keyser Run Fire Road. (Just before this turn, walled-in Bolen cemetery is on left.)

D   **4.4** Shortly after crossing gate, turn left into the parking lot. Little Devil Stairs Trail [blue-blazed] begins here (Elev 1200 ft), it's all uphill, 1700 ft climb, back to the trailhead.

B   **6.5** Back at Fourway, turn right onto Keyser Run Fire Road to begin final 200 ft ascent.

A   **7.5** Return to parking lot at Skyline Drive.

Directions for Piney Branch Circuit:

A   Follow directions for Little Devils Stairs Circuit.

B   **1.0** At Fourway junction, turn right onto Pole Bridge Link Trail [blue-blazed].
    1.5 As Sugarloaf Trail enters on right, continue on Pole Bridge Link Trail.

E   **1.9** Turn left onto blue-blazed Piney Branch Trail (Elev 2600 ft) and begin long descent that crosses Piney River twice.

K   **5.1** Go left on yellow-blazed Hull School Trail (Elev 1460 ft at junction).

C   **5.9** At concrete post for intersection with Keyser Run Fire Road, walled Bolen cemetery is on left. Go straight onto the yellow-blazed fire road and descend toward the Park boundary at SR 614.

D-A **7.0-10.1** Follow *Little Devils Stairs Circuit* directions.

Directions for Perimeter Circuit:

A-B Follow directions for Piney Branch Circuit to point [**E**].

E   **1.9** Go right onto Piney Branch Trail [blue-blazed].
    2.1 Cross Piney River and climb gently.

F   **3.3** Elevation 3085 ft. Turn left (south) onto AT [white-blazed].

G   **3.7** Pass trail leading left to Range View Cabin (available through reservations with PATC). Turn left on Piney Ridge Trail [blue-blazed], first following old roadbed, then veering right in 60 yd off road. Many storm blowdowns and efforts of volunteers to keep trail open are evident all around.

H   **5.7** Elevation 2300 ft. Pass Dwyer cemetery on right. In 90 yd, as Piney Ridge Trail turns sharply left, continue straight onto blue-blazed Fork Mtn Trail.

Range View Cabin

I   **7.0** Elevation 1630 ft. Turn left onto Hull School Trail [yellow-blazed] and descend toward Piney River.

J   **7.6** Elevation 1350 ft. Piney Branch Trail [blue-blazed] enters straight ahead on near side of stream. (Hull School Trail and Piney Branch Trail are concurrent here.) Turn left and ford Piney River to continue on Hull School Trail.

K   **7.7** Turn right on Hull School Trail at intersection where Piney Branch Trail goes straight.

C   **8.5** Elevation 1940 ft. At concrete marker for intersection with Keyser Run Fire Road, walled Bolen cemetery is on left. Go straight onto the yellow-blazed fire road and descend toward the Park boundary at SR 614.

D-A **9.6-12.7** Follow *Little Devils Stairs Circuit* directions.

Hike No. 5

MATHEWS ARM — OVERALL RUN

5

	Short Circuit	**Long Circuit**
Length:	8.0 mi	11.8 mi
Time Estimate:	4 hr 45 min	7 hr 30 min
Difficulty:	Moderate	Strenuous
Elev. Change:	1600 ft	2900 ft

Description: Both circuits go around Mathews Arm Campground, which is closed in colder months. If campground is open, hikers may park and start at map point C, near the registration office. This shortens each circuit by 2.2 mi (about an hour) and reduces the climb on each by 550 ft, by cutting out the A-B distance. When campground is closed, 0.7 mi entrance road is barred and access is from parking lot on Skyline Drive (map point A). Short Circuit covers moderate terrain near the campground. Long Circuit drops deep down Heiskell Hollow Trail into Overall Run Valley, then climbs back up Tuscarora-Overall Run Trail past Overall Run Falls. The uphill return is steep and long, but the falls and views are great – spectacular when cloaked in winter ice, and cooling on hot summer days. Pools near the lower elevation are big enough for dips. No pets are allowed on Traces Trail.

Access: Go to lot just south of Hogback Overlook and MP 21, on west side of the Drive. For shorter options available when campground is open, go to camp's entrance road on west side of Drive, 0.2 mi south of MP 22, and drive 0.7 mi down to campground registration station. Turn right just beyond the station, and right again into the parking lot.

<u>Short Circuit Directions:</u>
A   **0.0** Follow white-blazed AT south from parking area.

      0.3 At concrete signpost, turn right and descend on Tuscarora-Overall Run Trail (blue-blazed).

Also see PATC Map 9 (Grid E13)

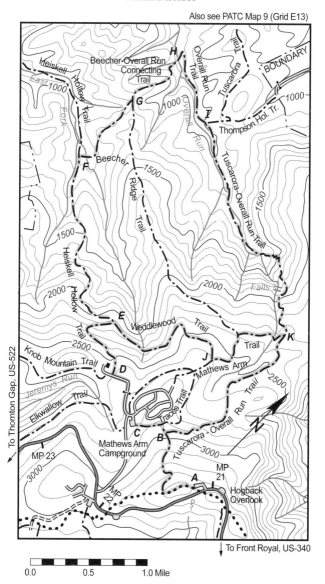

0.0   0.5   1.0 Mile

B   **1.1** As Tuscarora—Overall Run Trail goes right, bear left 100 yd, then go left on blue-blazed Traces Trail.

C   **1.6** At concrete marker at edge of parking lot [alternate starting point for 5.8 mi circuit] near camp registration office, angle right through lot past map board, then left on road at end of lot past another trailhead for Traces Trail.
1.7 Near registration station, go right and downhill on service road. Continue through loop in service road.
1.9 Following sign for Knob Mtn Trail, cross gate and continue downhill as road gets rougher.

D   **2.2** Turn right at concrete signpost onto Heiskell Hollow Trail [yellow-blazed].

E   **2.9** At next post, where Heiskell Hollow Trail cuts left, continue straight onto Weddlewood Trail [yellow-blazed].

J   **4.3** Turn left at concrete signpost onto Mathews Arm Trail [yellow-blazed].
4.8 Stay on Mathews Arm as Beecher Ridge Trail enters from left.

K   **5.3** At next concrete marker, turn right onto Tuscarora-Overall Run Trail [blue-blazed] and ascend.

B   **6.9** Where short spur trail goes right to Traces Trail, turn left to continue climbing Tuscarora-Overall Run Trail.
[To complete 5.8 mi alternate route from campground parking lot: Turn right for 100 yd, then left on blue-blazed Traces Trail and descend 0.5 mi to concrete post for point C in parking lot.]
7.7 Reach end of Tuscarora-Overall Run Trail near Skyline Drive and turn left on AT [white-blazed].

A   **8.0** Return to parking area and end hike.

__Long Circuit Directions__ – Distances from optional starting point C in parentheses:

A-D 0.0-2.2 Follow directions for Short Circuit. (For alternate route from point **C**, distance at point D is 0.6 mi.)

E   **2.9 (1.3)** Turn left onto Heiskell Hollow Trail [yellow-blazed] and begin long descent.

F **4.6 (3.0)** Turn right onto Beecher Ridge Trail [yellow-blazed] and cross small stream.

G **5.4 (3.8)** Turn left onto Beecher-Overall Run Connecting Trail [blue-blazed].

H **6.1 (7.7)** Ford Overall Run in flood-scoured, rocky area, go right at concrete post onto Overall Run Trail [blue-blazed], and begin long ascent along left bank of stream.
6.7 (8.3) Pass through open area where unmarked side trail goes right a short distance to swimming holes.

I **6.8 (8.4)** Go straight on Tuscarora-Overall Run Trail [blue-blazed] as Tuscarora-Thompson Hollow Trail goes left.

K **9.1 (10.7)** After steep, rocky, sometimes wet climb past spectacular waterfalls and great views over entire valley and west to Massanutten Mountain, continue straight on Tuscarora-Overall Run Trail as it passes turnoff to Mathews Arm Trail on right and leaves streamside.

If you started at point A:

B-A 10.7-11.8 Follow directions for Short Circuit.

If you started at point C:

B **(9.1)** Turn right for 100 yd, then turn left on blue-blazed Traces Trail and descend along slope above campground.

C **(9.6)** Finish at concrete post in campground parking lot.

Overall Run Falls

Hike No. 6
KNOB MOUNTAIN — NEIGHBOR MOUNTAIN AREA

6

	Jeremys Run— Neighbor Mtn Circuit	Knob Mtn— Jeremys Run Circuit
Length:	14.4 mi	13.1
Time Estimate:	8 hr 20 min	8 hr
Difficulty:	Strenuous	Strenuous
Elev. Change:	2600 ft	2900 ft

Description: Both circuits combine considerable climbs and descents with streambed hiking. The stream, Jeremys Run, is one of the most beautiful streams in the Park's North District. The circuits start at Elkwallow (2390 ft) and drop 1320 ft to the bottom of Jeremys Run, crossing the run 14 times. The Jeremys Run—Neighbor Mountain Circuit climbs from Jeremys Run to 2700 ft on Neighbor Mountain and then follows the AT back to Elkwallow. The Knob Mountain—Jeremys Run Circuit climbs to the peak of Knob Mountain (2865 ft), descends to Jeremys Run, and then climbs back to Elkwallow.

Access: Both circuits begin at Elkwallow Picnic Area, just south of Elkwallow Wayside near MP 24 on Skyline Drive. Park at the trailhead in the lot in the picnic area.

Jeremys Run—Neighbor Mountain Circuit Directions:
A **0.0** Follow trail 200 ft downhill from parking area to AT [white-blazed], just past comfort station. Continue straight (south), downhill, on AT.

B **0.3** Continue straight ahead, downhill, onto Jeremys Run Trail [blue-blazed], which enters where AT turns left. Veer left and come within sight of Jeremys Run.

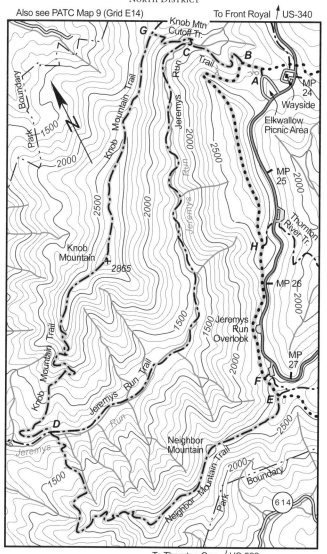

Also see PATC Map 9 (Grid E14)

To Front Royal ↑ US-340

Knob Mtn Cutoff Tr.

G

C

Knob Run Trail

B

A

MP 24

Wayside

Elkwallow Picnic Area

MP 25

Thornton River Tr.

Knob Mountain Trail

Jeremys Run

H

MP 26

Knob Mountain

2865

Jeremys Run Overlook

MP 27

F

E

Knob Mountain Trail

Jeremys Run Trail

Jeremys Run

D

Neighbor Mountain

Jeremys Run

Neighbor Mountain Trail

Park Boundary

614

To Thornton Gap / US-522

0.0   0.5   1.0 Mile

C **1.0** Pass concrete post at Knob Mtn Cutoff Trail [blue-blazed], which enters on right, and continue downstream on Jeremys Run Trail. Begin crossing and recrossing Jeremys Run.

5.2 Pass waterfall in Jeremys Run.

D **5.8** Turn left onto Neighbor Mtn Trail [yellow-blazed]. Climb via switchbacks to top of ridge. Watch for stands of white birch along the way.

8.6 Follow trail along crest of Neighbor Mtn over several small knobs which offer views in winter.

E **10.5** Turn left (north), downhill, onto AT. Spur trail straight ahead leads to Drive.

F **10.7** Continue downhill on AT past another spur trail to Drive. Soon begin long, steady climb.

H **12.0** Pass Thornton River Trail, which enters on right. (Thornton River Trail leads 0.3 mi to Drive, 0.4 mi south of MP 25.) Continue uphill on AT to high point west of Elkwallow and then descend.

B **14.2** Turn right (north), uphill, to stay on AT where Jeremys Run Trail goes left, downhill.

A **14.4** Where AT veers slightly left, continue straight ahead on spur trail. Arrive at parking area at lower end of picnic area.

Knob Mountain—Jeremys Run Circuit Directions:

A **0.0** Follow trail 200 ft downhill from parking area to AT [white-blazed], just past comfort station. Continue straight (south), downhill, on AT.

B **0.3** Continue straight ahead, downhill, onto Jeremys Run Trail [blue-blazed], which enters where AT turns left. Veer left and come within sight of Jeremys Run.

C **1.0** At concrete post, turn right onto Knob Mtn Cutoff Trail [blue-blazed]. Descend over boulders, cross Jeremys Run, and then climb, sometimes steeply.

G **1.6** Turn left onto Knob Mtn Trail [yellow-blazed].

3.8 Climb steadily to summit of Knob Mtn. Forest in this area has seen extensive gypsy moth damage.

4.7 Leave crest and drop 1600 ft to Jeremys Run via many switchbacks.

D **7.2** Ford Jeremys Run. Turn left, upstream, onto Jeremys Run Trail [blue-blazed]. In about 50 ft pass Neighbor Mtn Trail [yellow-blazed], which enters on right. Continue upstream on Jeremys Run Trail and begin crossing and recrossing Jeremys Run.

7.9 Pass waterfall.

C **12.1** Knob Mtn Cutoff Trail [blue-blazed] goes to left. Continue straight on Jeremys Run Trail uphill toward AT.

B **12.8** Continue straight uphill, as Jeremys Run Trail joins northbound AT.

A **13.1** Where AT veers slightly left, continue straight ahead on spur trail. Arrive at parking lot in picnic area.

Hike No. 7
ELKWALLOW WAYSIDE — MATHEWS ARM

7

Length:	6.0 mi
Time Estimate:	3 hr
Difficulty:	Easy
Elev. Change:	800 ft

Description: This hike uses the Knob Mtn and Elkwallow Trails for a circuit between Elkwallow Wayside and Mathews Arm Camp¬ground. The Wayside's restrooms, snack bar/cafeteria, store and gift shop -- open mid-April to late October -- provide conveniences for the hike. Mathews Arm Campground usually closes from mid-fall to late spring, and the access road from the Drive to trailheads near the campground parking lot usually closes with it. When it's open, starting at "G" is an option.

Access from Mathews Arm: Go 0.7 mi down the entrance road on west side of Skyline Drive, 0.2 mi south of MP 22, to campground registration station. Turn right just beyond registration station and right again into parking lot. Elkwallow trailhead is just across entrance road.

Access from Elkwallow Wayside: Turn into the Elkwallow Wayside parking lot at MP 24 on the west side of Skyline Drive. Find the concrete signpost for Elkwallow trailhead in the northeast corner of the lot.

Directions from Elkwallow Wayside:
A   **0.0**   Go north 125 yd on blue-blazed Elkwallow Trail, then go left at concrete marker to descend on white-blazed AT.

B   **0.4**   Continue downhill as unblazed trail joins on left from Elkwallow picnic area. (Wayside restrooms are locked in winter, but there are unlocked pit toilets 45 yd up this trail.)

34

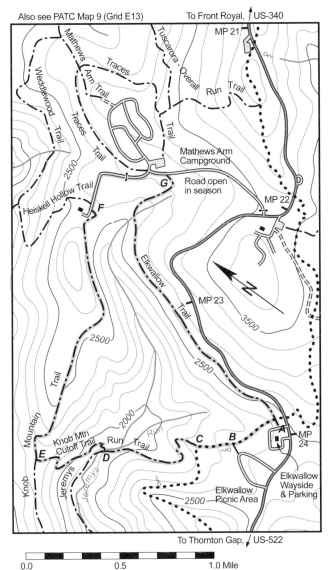

C **0.6** Another concrete post marks Jeremys Run Trail intersection, where AT turns left, uphill. Continue straight, now descending on Jeremys Run Trail [blue-blazed].

D **1.3** At next concrete post, turn right onto Knob Mountain Cutoff Trail [blue-blazed]. Descend, cross rocky streambed of Jeremys Run, then ascend the steep slope on narrow switchbacks with high gradient.

E **1.9** Turn right onto Knob Mtn Trail [yellow-blazed], still climbing. Trail becomes wide, grassy road on a broad ridge and, after 0.4 mi of moderate steepness, turns gently undulating. Pleasant hiking on cruise control through here.

3.5 Wastewater treatment plant is visible on left.

F **3.6** Bear right onto paved road. In 30 yd, pass concrete post on left marking Heiskell Hollow trailhead. Continue up steep paved road.

3.9 Step over chain gate and bear left on road. Bear right at a yield sign and follow exit roadway from campground.

G **4.2** 70 yd up road past campground registration station, turn right onto Elkwallow Trail [blue-blazed], initially on a wide and grassy roadbed. In 20 yd, turn right again at another concrete post and descend on a narrow, winding path. Cross drainage area on a long, wooden causeway. Climb 75 yd to a very wide road that descends gently.

A **6.0** After crossing white-blazed AT, continue another 125 yd on Elkwallow Trail to arrive back at parking area.

Hike No. 8

BYRDS NEST NO. 4

8

Length:	2.6 mi
Time Estimate:	1 hr 30 min
Difficulty:	Easy
Elev. Change:	750 ft

Description: This short, easy circuit passes Byrds Nest No. 4 —one of the four open-faced shelters donated to the Park by Virginia's late Senator Byrd. The shelter is for day use only and has no water supply, but it makes a decent spot for a picnic. The gentle grade along the Appalachian Trail, the mix of other trails used, the convenience of the shelter, good viewpoints, and proximity to the Drive along much of the circuit make this an excellent hike for families and first-timers.

Access: Go to paved parking area on east side of Skyline Drive 0.1 mi south of MP 28, just south of trailheads for Byrds Nest 4 access road (on west side of Drive) and Hull School Trail (on east side).

Directions:

A   0.0 From south end of parking lot, go south on Rocky Branch Trail [yellow-blazed], parallel with and close to Skyline Drive, initially through trees, then in open area with great views to the north and east.

B   0.4 Turn right onto white-blazed, northbound Appalachian Trail (AT), go 200 ft to Skyline Drive and angle left across it, still on AT.

C   0.6 Blue-blazed. 0.1 mi connector trail from Beahms Gap Overlook joins from right. Stay straight on AT.

0.7 Continue north.

0.8 Pass spring trail on left and continue through rocky open forest and climb Neighbor Mtn's ridge, where trees

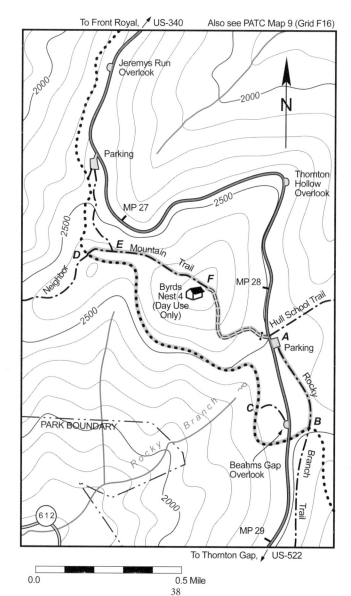

show gypsy moth damage.

D   **1.6** Turn right onto Neighbor Mtn Trail [yellow-blazed].

E   **1.7** Angle right to stay on Neighbor Mtn Trail. Connector trail that enters from left goes 0.3 mi to another parking area on Drive.

F   **2.3** Pass Byrd's Nest No. 4 shelter and descend steeply on access road [yellow-blazed] in front of shelter.

     2.5 Continue down access road to gate at Skyline Drive.

A   **2.6** Angle right across Skyline Drive parking to area and complete the circuit.

Large flowered trillium, photo by Lee Sheaffer

Hike No. 9
THORNTON HOLLOW

9

Length:	10.8 mi
Time Estimate:	7 hr
Difficulty:	Strenuous
Elev. Change:	2100 ft

Description: This circuit passes many reminders of the people who inhabited these mountains before the Park was established. It passes through old homesteads and the Dwyer cemetery, which contains grave sites dating from the 1800s. In early spring the lower end of Thornton River Trail has a profusion of flowering redbud. The two biggest climbs along this circuit (800 ft near the start, between Jeremys Run and Range View Cabin, and another 1000 ft on the last leg between the Hull School/Thornton River Trail intersection and Skyline Drive) are broken by a long downhill along the Ridge, Fork Mountain and Hull School Trails.

Access from Skyline Drive: Go 0.4 mi south of MP 25 and park in lot on east side of Drive. Cross Drive to begin circuit from west side.

Directions:
- **A** **0.0** Cross Drive (Elevation 2260 ft) diagonally to left and climb via switch-backs.
- **B** **0.4** Turn right (north) onto AT [white-blazed] and hike through stand of evergreens.
- **C** **2.6** At junction with Jeremys Run Trail [blue-blazed], turn sharply right to stay on AT and start gentle climb from 2220 ft elevation. Bear left at both forks. (First fork leads to Elkwallow Picnic Area, second fork right leads to

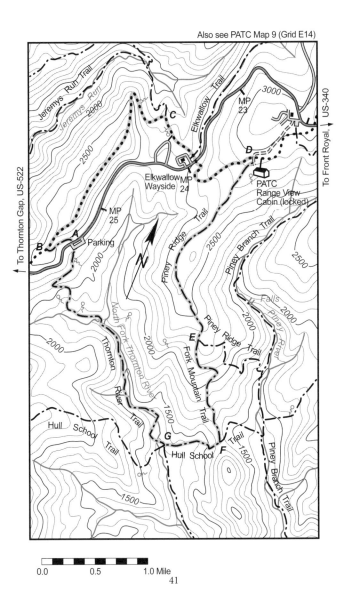

Elkwallow Wayside.)

3.0 Pass Elkwallow Trail [blue-blazed] and stay on AT 100 ft to Drive. Cross Drive, still climbing as trail bears left.

D **3.9** Turn right onto Range View Cabin service road (elev 3000 ft). Go 60 yards, and veer right again onto Piney Ridge Trail [blue-blazed]. (Service road continues short distance to Range View Cabin and spring 30 yd in front of cabin. This cabin is locked -- available for use through advance reservations with the PATC.) Descend on Piney Ridge Trail.

E **6.0** Continue straight onto Fork Mtn Trail [blue-blazed] where Piney Ridge Trail turns sharply left. (Old cemetery is on right 90 yd before this intersection.)

F **7.2** Turn right onto Hull School Trail [yellow-blazed].

G **7.8** Elevation 1275 ft. Bear right onto Thornton River Trail [yellow-blazed to left, blue-blazed to right] and follow blue- blazes. Hull School, a local primary school, was located here. Begin long ascent from 1275 ft elevation along North Fork of Thornton River, crossing river four times. Valley is wide here, with many indications of old homesteads, old roads and remains of a Model A Ford which may be obscured by brush in the summer. As valley narrows, climb gently but steadily upward through open woods.

A **10.8** Arrive back at parking area.

Hike No. 10
HAZEL COUNTRY

10

	Pine Hill Gap- Broad Hollow	Catlett Mtn- Short Mtn
Length:	6.1 mi	8.5 mi
Time Estimate:	3 hr 45 min	5 hr
Difficulty:	Moderate	Strenuous
Elev. Change:	1600 ft	2400 ft

Description: This area, between the Hazel and Hughes Rivers, was well settled before the Park was established. Now, its old farm roads have become part of a complex network of trails. Most remaining farm buildings burned in 2000, when fire swept nearly all of Hazel Country. Look closely for lonely chimneys, old apple orchards, crumbling stone walls, and fields returning to forest. The moderate Pine Hill Gap—Broad Hollow Circuit passes some ruins spared by the fire. The Catlett Mtn—Short Mtn Circuit circles the namesake mountain pair, descends along the flank of Hot Mountain to Nicholson Hollow, and climbs up Hannah Run. Along the way, it passes several burned-out ruins.

Access to Pine Hill Gap—Broad Hollow Circuit: Take US 522 to SR 231 (0.8 mi south of Sperryville and 12.7 mi north of Madison). Go south 3.3 mi on SR 231. Just before bridge over Hazel River, turn right onto SR 681. Follow SR 681 2.7 mi to its end – past SR 600, which enters from right at 1.1 mi and through a hard left at 2.5 mi., then a hard right. Park on left side at end of SR 681, just past old red and white trailer. On weekends, parking is also permitted in the school bus turn-around near the hard left at the 2.5 mi point. **Park at your own risk – There is no Park security here, and you risk being towed if you park outside the very limited area designated.**

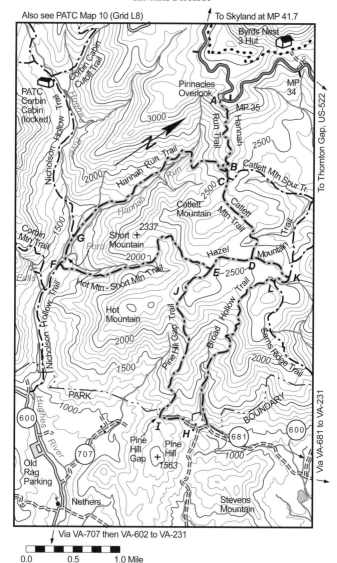

Pine Hill Gap—Broad Hollow Circuit Directions:

H   **0.0** From concrete post at end of SR 681 that gives distance to Pine Hill Gap Trail as 0.3 mi, hike up former roadbed. Road turns rocky and follows Park boundary.

I   **0.5** At concrete post turn right onto Pine Hill Gap Trail [yellow-blazed] and climb. This trail follows the route of Old Hazel Road, the earliest road serving the Hazel Country community, possibly dating from the late 18th century. It connected Nethers to Lee Highway.

J   **2.2** Concrete post on left marks former trail to Hot Mountain summit.

E   **2.5** Hot-Short Mtn Trail [blue-blazed] enters on left at concrete post. Continue straight on Hazel Mtn Trail [yellow-blazed].

D   **3.0** Pass Catlett Mtn Trail [blue-blazed], which enters on left at concrete post, and keep on Hazel Mtn Trail.

K   **3.5** Turn right at concrete post onto Broad Hollow Trail [blue-blazed]. Hazel School, which served this area before SNP was established, stood on west side of this intersection. Spring is 200 ft downhill to right of this junction. The original Old Hazel Road continued to the left, following White Rocks Trail before dropping down Beech Hollow to Lee Highway.

L   **3.7** At concrete post where Sams Ridge Trail goes left, turn right and continue on Broad Hollow Trail to begin 1400 ft descent to SR 681.

     4.4 Pass cabin remains on left.

     4.9 Homesite with split chestnut siding still stands to right of trail. October 2000 fire jumped this part of the hollow.

     5.2 Pass homesite on right and begin final descent toward trailhead, with three crossings of Broad Hollow Run.

     5.9 Reach SR 681 and turn right to walk long road

H   **6.1** Reach parking area at end of road to complete circuit.

Access to Catlett—Short Mountain Circuit: Park at Pinnacles Overlook on east side of Skyline Drive, 0.2 mi south of MP 35.

Catlett Mountain—Short Mountain Circuit Directions:

A   **0.0** From north end of Pinnacles Overlook on Skyline Drive, begin descent on Hannah Run Trail.

B   **1.0** At concrete post in deep hollow, turn left onto Catlett Mountain Trail [blue-blazed] in old roadbed.

C   **1.1** At concrete marker for intersection with Catlett Mtn Spur Trail [blue-blazed], turn right to stay on Catlett Mtn Trail. Bear right around pit and past remnants of stone wall. Here, settlerNathan Jenkins dug unsuccessfully for gold in late 19th and early 20th centuries. Cross Catlett Mtn shoulder, descend gently through pines and abandoned orchard. Cross stream and climb.

1.2 Pass new mountain laurel growth, marking re-covery from October 2000 fire.

D   **2.2** At concrete post, turn right onto Hazel Mtn Trail [yellow-blazed].

E   **2.8** Turn right again at next concrete post onto Hot-Short Mtn Trail [blue-blazed] and descend. Shortly, note stone chimney to left, with iron swing-out for cookpot support.

3.4 Pass chimney on right, then cross stream.

3.7 More homesite ruins on left.

3.9 More ruins across Hogback Run on right, with concrete trough.

F   **4.8** At concrete post (Elev 1200 ft], turn right onto blue-blazed Nicholson Hollow Trail and begin ascent along Hughes River.

4.9 Ford Hannah Run and Church Run at old bridge site.

G   **5.1** Turn right at concrete post onto Hannah Run Trail [blue-blazed] and cross Church Run. Nicholson Hollow School and Hughes River Church once stood here. Continue climbing, passing many stone chimneys and foundations in next 1.7 mi on both sides of trail.

5.4 Note two stone chimneys on right, across Hannah Run, and large white pines in this area. The pines date from 1936 when open fields were allowed to reforest.

6.9 Cross Hannah Run headwaters in ravine and begin-steep climb.

B   **7.5**   At concrete post in hollow, turn left to stay on Hannah Run Trail and continue climbing toward Skyline Drive.

A   **8.5**   Reach Drive and end hike at Pinnacles Overlook.

Stony Man Mountain

Hike No. 11
STONY MAN MOUNTAIN

11

Length:	3.4 mi
Time Estimate:	1 hr 45 min
Difficulty:	Easy
Elev. Change:	370 ft

Description: This is one of the most scenic circuits in the Park, with mostly well maintained and marked trails. Grades are not difficult. Although Stony Man (4011 ft) is the second highest peak in the Park, the climb from the parking lot is only about 330 ft. Outstanding panoramas from Stony Man and Little Stony Man range from Shenandoah Valley and Massanutten Mountain in the west to the Piedmont in the east. Passamaquoddy Trail was laid out in 1932 by George Freeman Pollock, founder of Skyland and a "self-made legend" according to author Henry Heatwole. Pollock claimed Passamaquoddy was an Indian word for "abounding in pollock (a kind of fish)," but he may have twisted the meaning. A copper mine near the summit of Stony Man played out in 1883, at a depth of 100 ft. This circuit can be accessed from either of two points on Skyline Drive that are two miles apart. Trail directions are from the southern access point. **No pets are allowed on Stony Man Trail, except dogs with through-hikers on the stretch shared with the AT.**

Access from south: Use northern entrance of Skyland, just south of MP 41 on west side of Skyline Drive. This turnoff is the highest point on the Drive (3680 ft). Park in Stony Man Trail Parking Area on right (point [A] on the map).

Access from north: Go to Little Stony Man Parking Area, just south of MP 39 on west side of Drive. This parking area ([F] on trail map) only accommodates a few cars. Take spur trail from lower end of parking area to AT [white- blazed] and turn left. Begin circuit at [D]. (Circuit length from north is 4.2 mi.)

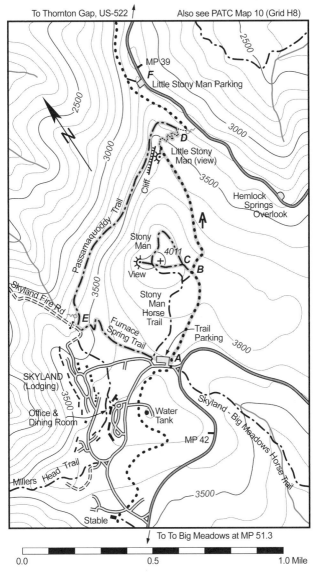

To Thornton Gap, US-522

Also see PATC Map 10 (Grid H8)

MP 39
F
Little Stony Man Parking

2500

3000

N

D
Little Stony Man (view)

Cliff

3000

3500

Hemlock Springs Overlook

Passamaquoddy Trail

Stony Man
4011
View
C
B

3500

Stony Man Horse Trail

Skyland Fire Rd

3500

E

Furnace Spring Trail

Trail Parking
A
3800

SKYLAND (Lodging)

Office & Dining Room

Water Tank

MP 42

Skyland - Big Meadows Horse Trail

3500

Millers Head Trail

3500

Stable

To To Big Meadows at MP 51.3

0.0   0.5   1.0 Mile

Directions:

A **0.0** From right side of Stony Man Trailhead Parking Area, follow white-blazed AT north. Stony Man Trail [blue-blazed] initially shares trail with AT [white-blazed].

B **0.4** At the trail intersection (marked with a double white-blaze and trail post), continue straight (west) toward Stony Man summit on blue-blazed trail. (AT goes off to right.)

C **0.5** Shortly, the trail splits again. Ignore yellow-blazed Stony Man Horse Trail and take blue-blazed summit loop trail (0.4 mi) in either direction. From the top, cliffs offer incredible views. Return to AT after completing the loop.

B **1.0** Turn left (north) onto white-blazed AT and descend.
1.6 Little Stony Man cliffs afford fantastic view of Shenandoah Valley. Continue down AT toward intersection with Passamaquoddy Trail.

D **1.9** Turn left onto blue-blazed Passamaquoddy Trail, which leads to another bare rock outcrop with yet another view of the valley before curving left (south) on a ledge along the western slope of Stony Man.
2.3 Rocky stretches in slide area require careful footing.

E **2.9** At concrete post, Passamaquoddy Trail meets Skyland Fire Road at Furnace Spring. Turn left onto the Fire Road at this marker and quickly left again at next concrete marker for Furnace Spring Trail {yellow-blazed]. At first, Furnace Spring Trail heads back east, upslope from and parallel to Passamaquoddy Trail. Then it swings back to the right (south) as it winds among the trees and up the ridge, picking its way over rocks.

A **3.4** Angle left at T intersection and, in about 100 yd, return to trailhead parking lot.

Hike No. 12
NICHOLSON HOLLOW —
CORBIN CABIN

12

Length:	4.1 mi
Time Estimate:	2 hr 30 min
Difficulty:	Moderate
Elev. Change:	1100 ft

Description: Briars, shrubs, trees and past fires have obscured many signs of the mountain settlements that existed when the Park was created. Nicholson Hollow has SNP's largest concentration of fences, chimneys, and foundations -- all reminders of the families who once lived and worked here. This circuit descends from Skyline Drive to Corbin Cabin, where George Corbin built a typical place in pre-Park days. The cabin has been restored by PATC and is available for use through advance reservation. The path down to the cabin is a smooth downhill, but the trail back up to Skyline Drive is quite steep, rising 1000 ft in 1.5 mi.

Access: Go to parking area just north of MP 38 on west side of Skyline Drive.

Directions:

A 0.0 The AT [white-blazed] parallels the rear edge of the parking area just a few feet into the woods via the Corbin Cabin Cutoff Trail. Turn left onto the AT and follow it to the left (south).

B 0.7 Turn left at concrete post onto Crusher Ridge Trail [blue-blazed]. Turn left at next concrete post onto Nicholson Hollow Trail [blue-blazed].

C 0.8 Cross Drive diagonally to left and find continuation of Nicholson Hollow Trail 100 yd to the north. The trail descends on an old roadbed through an area of scrub oak and laurel.

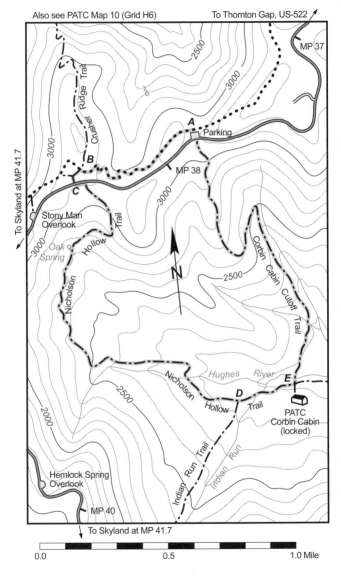

Also see PATC Map 10 (Grid H6)

To Thornton Gap, US-522

MP 37

Crusher Ridge Trail

2500

3000

A

Parking

To Skyland at MP 41.7

3000

B

MP 38

C

3000

Stony Man Overlook

Oak Spring

Nicholson Hollow Trail

3000

N

2500

Corbin Cabin Cutoff Trail

Hughes River

E

D

Nicholson Hollow Trail

PATC Corbin Cabin (locked)

2500

Indian Run Trail

Indian Run

Hemlock Spring Overlook

2000

MP 40

To Skyland at MP 41.7

0.0   0.5   1.0 Mile

1.2 Pass the walled-in Dale Spring to the right of the trail.

2.4 Cross Hughes River.

D **2.6** Pass the concrete post marking Indian Run Trail [blue-blazed], which enters on the right in remains of a hemlock forest, and shortly after cross Indian Run. Hemlocks throughout the Park have been killed by an Asian insect called the woolly adelgid in recent years. Continue on Nicholson Hollow Trail.

E **2.7** Corbin Cabin is on right. At the concrete post in front of the cabin, turn left onto the Corbin Cabin Cutoff Trail and cross the Hughes River.

3.3 Trail becomes steep, then switchbacks left.

A **4.1** Cross Skyline Drive to parking area and end hike.

Corbin Cabin

Hike No. 13
OLD RAG MOUNTAIN

13

Length:	9.4 mi
Time Estimate:	6 hr
Difficulty:	Strenuous
Elev. Change:	2200 ft

Description: Old Rag (3291 ft) is the most spectacular mountain in the northern Virginia Blue Ridge. Unlike most mountains in the Blue Ridge, it stands alone as an outlier rather than as part of a continuous chain. It is popular in all seasons and particularly crowded on weekends. Old Rag's attractions include a rugged scramble among boulders and through a narrow crevice in the granite near the top. From the summit and several false summits en route, there are great all-around views. Spring offers displays of wild flowers, trilliums, dogwood, and redbud. Two day-use shelters along the way facilitate picnics: Byrds Nest No. 1 and Old Rag Shelter. Camping is not permitted at either shelter, or elsewhere on the mountain above 2800 ft. This hike is strenuous and hikers should carry ample water. **Pets are not permitted on Old Rag's Ridge Trail or Saddle Trail.**

Access: Take US 522 to SR 231, which is 0.8 mi south of Sperryville, Va., and 12.7 mi north of Madison, Va. Go south 8.3 mi on SR 231, cross Hughes River, and immediately turn right (west) onto SR 602. Stay on left side of Hughes River. Route number changes to 601, 707, and then 600. Do not cross Hughes River. After 3.5 mi from SR 231, just beyond Nethers, Va., an SNP parking area accommodates 200 cars. Park here and pay fee. Plan early arrival (before 10 am) on weekends and throughout October. When lot is full, no more permits are issued and no roadside parking allowed beyond the lot.

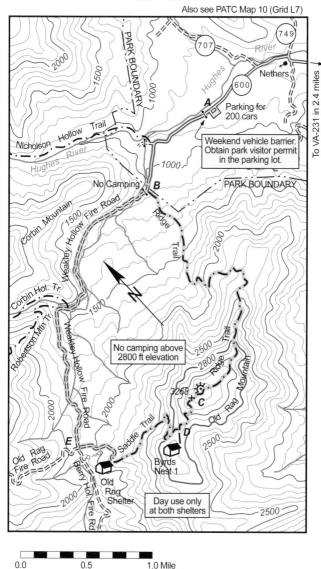

Directions:

A   **0.0**   After checking in with Park staff, begin hike on SR 600, following Hughes River then Brokenback Run upstream.

B   **0.8** At the far end of a restricted parking area at end of SR 600, turn left onto Ridge Trail [blue-blazed] and climb through forest with many switchbacks.

    3.0 Flexibility and strength help to go over, under, around boul-ders, and squeeze through cracks in rock and follow blue-blazes closely.

C   **4.1**   Reach summit. Ridge Trail turns into Saddle Trail at sign. Turn right onto spur to summit vistas. After exploring summit and its great views, return to this point. To continue down mountain, follow Saddle Trail [blue-blazed].

D   **4.6**   At signpost just before Byrds Nest Shelter No. 1, turn right to stay on Saddle Trail.

    4.9   Turn sharply right to leave ridge and descend steadily by switchbacks.

    5.6 As Old Rag Shelter comes into view (100 ft ahead), turn right onto Old Rag Fire Road. Small spring is down-hill from front of shelter.

E   **6.1**   Signpost marks junction of three yellow-blazed fire roads—Weakley Hollow, Berry Hollow, and Old Rag. Take sharp right onto Weakley Hollow Fire Road and descend.

    7.2   Pass Robertson Mtn Trail and Corbin Hollow Trail, which come in from left.

    7.4 Cross large metal bridge over Brokenback Run.

    8.5 Cross series of footbridges over Brokenback Run and ford Chris Branch.

B-A 8.6-9.4   Return to parking area on SR 600.

Old Rag Mountain

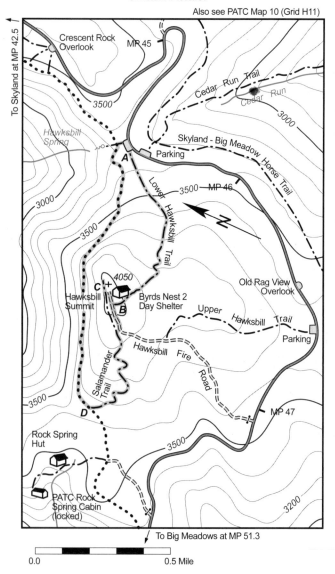

Hike No. 14

HAWKSBILL MOUNTAIN

14

Length:	2.9 mi
Time Estimate:	1 hr 45 min
Difficulty:	Easy
Elev. Change:	750 ft

Description: This circuit begins with a sometimes steep climb from Hawksbill Gap parking area (3365 ft) to the top of Hawksbill, the highest peak in the Park (4051 ft). Around the peak, there is a viewing platform with a 270 degree vista, majestic bluffs, and the appropriately named Byrd's Nest Shelter No. 2. The nearby area serves as a base for a raptor restoration program. Birds of prey and vultures may be seen around the peak. The shelter is day use only. A winding descent through woodlands along the Salamander Trail may turn up red-backed salamanders, the trail's namesake, under rocks and logs. Finally, a gentle descent along the AT on Hawksbill's north-facing flank returns to the trailhead. No camping is permitted on Hawksbill Mtn. above 3600 ft.

Access: 0.6 mi south of MP 45, turn into the Hawksbill Gap Parking Area on the west side of Skyline Drive.

Directions:

A **0.0** Take the Lower Hawksbill Trail [blue-blazed] past the map and information board at rear of lot.

B **0.7** Pass concrete post and turn right on Hawksbill Fire Road toward Byrds Nest 2 shelter.

C **0.8** Continue past the shelter, where road ends, to reach the stone-walled observation platform at the peak. Great views span the most of the horizon.

B **0.9** Return to the concrete post on the fire road. Continue down the road 100 yd, then turn right onto Salamander Trail [blue-blazed], which shortly veers left and downhill.

.8 After descent through well shaded woods, turn right onto white-blazed AT and begin gentler descent.

2.3 Pass talus slope with impressive boulders.

2.8 At concrete post, turn right onto access trail for Hawksbill Gap parking.

A 2.9 End hike at Hawksbill Parking Area.

Hawksbill Mountain Observation Platform

Hike No. 15

CEDAR RUN — WHITEOAK CANYON

15

	Short Circuit	*Long Circuit*
Length:	8.3 mi	9.6 mi
Time Estimate:	6 hr	6 hr 30 min
Difficulty:	Strenuous	Strenuous
Elev. Change:	2800 ft	3200 ft

Description: These circuits go through two of the deepest and steepest ravines in SNP, and both feature substantial elevation changes. Both ravines have views of waterfalls, cascades, and high cliffs. The waterfalls are especially spectacular when ice-covered in winter. Both circuits ascend Whiteoak Canyon, then descend Cedar Run Canyon. The Short Circuit climbs the steepest part of Whiteoak, then uses Whiteoak Road and Skyland-Big Meadows Horse Trail to cut over to Cedar Run. The Long Circuit goes higher up Whiteoak Canyon to the Limberlost and crosses Skyline Drive for views to the west before descending along Cedar Run. Limberlost features a once-beautiful hemlock forest that has been destroyed by an invasive insect. It is now a case study in transitional vegetation. The circuits can be hiked from the Park's eastern boundary or from Skyline Drive at the Hawksbill Parking Area, just south of MP 45. Directions are from the Park boundary. **Pets are not permitted on the Limberlost Trail.**

Access from Park Boundary: **If coming from the north,** go to intersection of US 211 and US 522/SR 231 in Sperryville, and follow SR 231 south 0.8 mi. Turn right to stay on SR 231 (F.T. Valley Rd). At 11 mi from starting point, turn right onto SR 643 (Etlan Rd). At 15.3 mi, turn right onto SR 600 (Weakley Hollow Rd). Parking area is on left at 19 mi. **From the south and east,** follow SR 231 to SR 670 (about 5 mi north of Madison), turn west onto SR 670 and pass Criglersville. About 5 mi

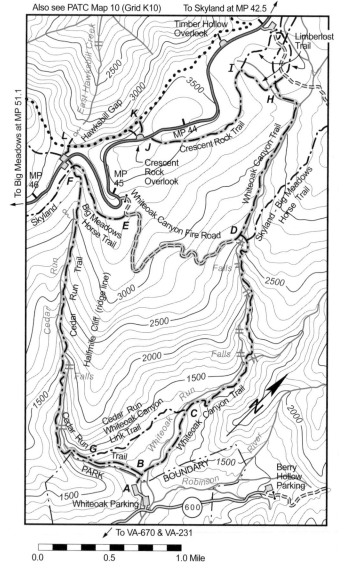

Also see PATC Map 10 (Grid K10)   To Skyland at MP 42.5

Timber Hollow Overlook

Limberlost Trail

To Big Meadows at MP 51.1

East Hawksbill Creek

Hawksbill Gap

MP 44

Crescent Rock Trail

K

J

Crescent Rock Overlook

MP 45

MP 46

Skyland

Whiteoak Canyon Fire Road

Whiteoak Canyon Trail

Skyland - Big Meadows Horse Trail

Big Meadows Horse Trail

E

Falls

D

Cedar Run

Cedar Run Trail

Halfmile Cliff (ridge line)

Falls

Cedar Run Whiteoak Canyon Link Trail

Whiteoak Run

Falls

Whiteoak Canyon Trail

C

G

Cedar Run Trail

B

PARK   BOUNDARY

Robinson River

Berry Hollow Parking

A

Whiteoak Parking

To VA-670 & VA-231

0.0   0.5   1.0 Mile

mi, turn left onto SR 600, and follow north along Robinson River for 3.6 mi. Just beyond point where road crosses Cedar Run, turn left into large parking area divided into two sections by low water bridge. Trailhead is at end of parking area farthest from SR 600. Check in and pay entrance fee. **This access area may be filled, especially on weekends.**

Access from Skyline Drive: Park at Hawksbill Gap Parking Area, just south of MP 45. Cross Drive and begin circuit at [**F**] on Cedar Run Trail. At [**B**], turn left up Whiteoak Canyon.

Short Circuit Directions:

A **0.0** (Elevation 1180 ft) Take Whiteoak Canyon Trail [blue-blazed] from SR 600 parking lot. Cross bridge over Cedar Run.

B **0.1** (Elevation 1200 ft) Pass Cedar Run Trail [blue-blazed], which enters on left, and ford Whiteoak Run.

C **0.7** Cedar Run-Whiteoak Canyon Link Trail [blue-blazed] enters on left. Camping is prohibited on Whiteoak Canyon Trail between here and Skyline Drive. Continue climbing on Whiteoak Canyon Trail. Come close to Whiteoak Run.
1.4 Cross small creek that enters on right.
1.5 Falls, on stream just passed, are visible on right. Begin steep ascent along northeast side of Whiteoak Run. Occasional views of waterfalls appear as trail switchbacks up canyon.
2.7 Spur trail leads left 250 ft to base of uppermost falls.
2.8 Excellent view to left overlooks upper Whiteoak Falls. Continue straight as yellow-blazed trail enters from right.

D **2.9** Turn left onto Skyland—Big Meadows Horse Trail [yellow-blazed] and ford Whiteoak Run (Elev 2600 ft). If the creek is too high here, continue upstream a few yd, cross-over footbridge, and return downstream to yellow-blazed trail. Skyland-Big Meadows Horse Trail follows Whiteoak Fire Road uphill, now heading west on easier grade.

E **4.5** (Elevation 3450 ft) At fork where Fire Road goes right, turn left and continue on Skyland—Big Meadows Horse Trail.

F **5.1** Take sharp left on blue-blazed Cedar Run Trail and descend into ravine.

    6.1 Uppermost waterfall on Cedar Run is visible to right.

    6.6 Ford stream and climb opposite bank of ravine.

    6.8 Approach Cedar Run again. Tallest cascade on Cedar Run is to left. Sheer Halfmile Cliffs are across the stream.

    7.5 Turn left and ford Cedar Run immediately below falls. (Don't follow bed of old road that continues downstream.)

G **7.8** (Elevation 1530 ft) At fork, bear right to stay on Cedar Run Trail; Cedar Run-Whiteoak Canyon Link Trail [blue-blazed] enters on left.

B **8.2** Turn right onto Whiteoak Canyon Trail [blue-blazed], cross bridge over Cedar Run, and continue downhill.

A **8.3** Return to parking area just off SR 600 and end hike.

Long Circuit Directions:

A-C Follow directions for Short Circuit.

D **2.9** Cross bridge over Whiteoak Run (a few yd upstream of ford), go right and keep climbing Whiteoak Canyon Trail.

H **4.3** Turn left onto Limberlost Trail.

I **4.7** Turn left onto Crescent Rock Trail [blue-blazed]. (This intersection is 50 ft before boardwalk on Limberlost Trail.)

J **5.7** (Elevation 3625 ft) Cross Drive at Crescent Rock Overlook and follow entrance road downhill to parking area. At parking area, take access trail a few ft north of overlook, turn left and descent to AT.

K **5.9** Turn left (south) onto AT [white-blazed].

L **6.3** At concrete post, turn left, uphill, onto spur trail to Drive at Hawksbill Gap Parking Area. Cross Drive and start down Cedar Run Trail [blue-blazed] on east slope.

F **6.4** (Elevation 3375 ft) Stay on Cedar Run Trail as it crosses Skyland—Big Meadows Horse Trail [yellow-blazed], and continue descent into Cedar Run Canyon.

7.4 Uppermost waterfall on Cedar Run is visible to right.

7.9 Ford stream and climb opposite bank of ravine.

8.1 Approach Cedar Run again. Tallest cascade on Cedar Run is to left and sheer Halfmile Cliffs are across creek.

8.9 Turn left and ford Cedar Run immediately below falls. (Don't follow bed of old road that continues downstream.)

G-A 9.1 - 9.6 *Follow directions for Short Circuit.*

Redback Mountain Salamander

Hike No. 16

DARK HOLLOW FALLS — UPPER ROSE RIVER

16

	Short Circuit	*Long Circuit*
Length:	3.9 mi	6.4 mi
Time Estimate:	2 hr 30 min	4 hr
Difficulty:	Easy	Moderate
Elev. Change:	900 ft	1400 ft

Description: Both circuits travel along Rose River and Hog-camp Branch on the east side of Skyline Drive, across from Big Meadows Campground. Both pass Rose River Falls and the site of an old copper mine, traces of which have nearly been erased by erosion. The Long Circuit – or a brief side trip off the Short Circuit -- adds Dark Hollow Falls. The longer circuit also offers good views from the Appalachian Trail as it circles the Big Meadows picnic and camping areas west of the Drive, and it uses the Story of the Forest Trail, a trail through botanically interesting wetland. **Pets are not permitted on Story of the Forest Trail or Dark Hollow Falls Trail.**

Access to Short Circuit: Park on west side of Skyline Drive at Fishers Gap, just south of MP 49.

Access to Long Circuit: Drive to Big Meadows, just south of MP 51 on Skyline Drive. Turn in and follow signs to Amphitheater Parking Area.

Directions for Short Circuit:

D **0.0** From Fishers Gap Parking Area (Elevation 3060 ft), cross Drive onto Rose River Fire Road [yellow-blazed]. Shortly, the Skyland-Big Meadows Horse Trail [also yellow-blazed] enters on left and then exits on right. Stay on the Fire Road as it descends, heading south.

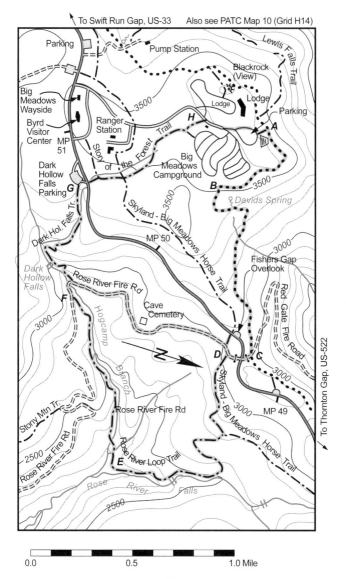

0.0   0.5   1.0 Mile

Pass cave cemetery on right.

F **1.2** Just before bridge over Hogcamp Branch, Dark Hollow Falls Trail [blue-blazed] enters on right. ***For side trip to Dark Hollow Falls:*** Turn right onto Dark Hollow Falls Trail and go 0.2 mi to falls (0.4 mi round trip). ***To continue circuit:*** Stay on Rose River Fire Road 50 ft past bridge to concrete post that marks another intersection, and turn left off Fire Road onto Rose River Loop Trail [blue-blazed] to descend along Hogcamp Branch.

E **2.3** (Elevation 2250 ft) Turn sharply left, cross footbridge and then swing away from Hogcamp Branch. In 100 yd, pass hard-to-spot site of old copper mine to left of trail. Approach Rose River. At concrete post, turn left and begin to climb.

3.0 Now heading north/uphill, pass falls of Rose River on right (a 25-ft drop to a deep pool).

3.3 Turn left, uphill, onto Skyland—Big Meadows Horse Trail [yellow-blazed], which is in old roadbed.

D **3.9** Turn right onto Rose River Fire Road [yellow-blazed] at Fishers Gap just below Drive, and return to Fishers Gap Parking Area to complete the hike.

Directions for Long Circuit:

A **0.0** From lower end of Big Meadows Amphitheater Parking Area (Elevation 3600 ft), walk downhill to find AT [white-blazed] and turn right (north) onto AT.

0.3 Follow AT as it swings right. Big Meadows Campground is now on right. Openings along AT give good views north and west.

B **0.6** Stay on AT through sharp left at concrete post. Davids Spring is 50 ft left of trail.

1.5 Go straight across clearing with blooming hepatica in spring and clematis in summer.

C **1.6** Turn right on Red Gate Rd. In 350 ft, cross Drive.

D **1.7** On west side of Drive (Elev 3060), go left off road onto Skyland—Big Meadows Horse Trail [yellow-blazed] and head downhill.

2.2 Go right on Rose River Loop Trail descend [blue-blazed] and. Rose River appears on left after a few turns.

2.6 To continue circuit, follow Loop Trail as it turns sharply right, away from falls, but still follows river downstream.

E **3.3** Past concrete post (Elevation 2250 ft), trail leaves Rose River and passes faint tailings and ruins of copper mine.

3.5 Cross footbridge over Hogback Branch. Veer right on Rose River Loop Trail, to climb along Hogback Branch.

F **4.4** Turn right at concrete post onto Rose River Fire Road [yellow-blazed], cross bridge over Hogcamp Branch and turn left onto Dark Hollow Falls Trail [blue-blazed]. Climb steeply via switchbacks 0.2 mi to Dark Hollow Falls (series of terraced cascades), then continue uphill.

G **5.3** Reach Drive by parking area (Elevation 3450 ft) and go straight across. In 100 yd, angle right onto Story of the Forest Trail [blue-blazed]. The left fork over Stonebridge goes to Byrd Visitor Center.

5.5 Pass Skyland-Big Meadows horse trail [yellow-blazed].

5.9 Turn left to continue on Story of the Forest Trail. The other fork goes to Big Meadows Camp-ground.

Dark Hollow Falls

H **6.1** Trail ends at paved entrance road to Big Meadows picnic and camping areas. Turn right onto paved path to Amphitheater Parking Area.

A **6.4** Complete circuit at Amphitheater Parking Area.

Hike No. 17
RAPIDAN CAMP

17

Length: 7.7 mi
Time Estimate: 5 hr
Difficulty: Moderate
Elev. Change: 1200 ft

Description: President Herbert Hoover created the complex of rustic cabins featured on this circuit, which served as a summer White House from 1929-33 (before President Roosevelt created Camp David in Maryland's Catoctin Mountains). Hoover used the camp for work as well as relaxation. Three of the original cabins remain today. The Brown House, used by the President and his wife, Lou Henry Hoover, has been rehabilitated to its appearance in the 1930s and is open for tours by reservation. The Prime Minister, used by Britain's Prime Minister Ramsay MacDonald while visiting Hoover, today contains exhibits telling the story of Rapidan Camp. Volunteer caretakers from late May through mid-October welcome visitors to the camp.

Access: Go to Milam Gap Parking lot, MP 52.6 on west side of Skyline Drive.

Directions:
A **0.0** From Milam Gap Parking lot, cross drive on AT.
B **0.1** At concrete post turn left on Mill Prong Trail [blueblazed], and descend gently.
  0.6 Cross Mill Prong Creek.
C **1.0** Horse trail from Rapidan Fire Road enters from left. Trail is now yellow-blazed. Back country camping is prohibited from here to Rapidan Camp.
  1.3 Pass Big Rock Falls.
D **1.7** Turn right at access road and then left to enter the

Also see PATC Map 10 (Grid I16)

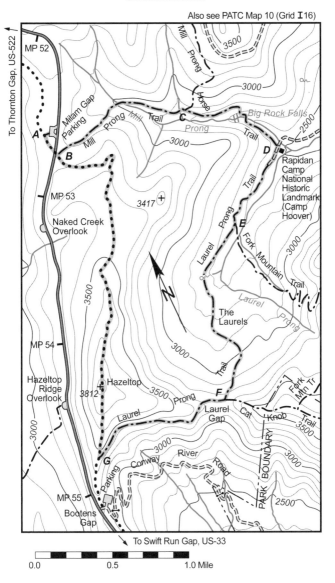

0.0   0.5   1.0 Mile

camp. Creel House is on the left. Spend time enjoying the exhibits in the Prime Minister's House. Continue through the camp and follow the Laurel Prong Trail [yellow-blazed], on the old forest road.

E **2.6** Fork Mountain Trail [yellow-blazed] enters from left. Remain on Laurel Prong Trail, now blue-blazed and begin to climb.

F **3.8** Reach Saddle and Cat Knob Trail on left. Turn right on Laurel Prong Trail and continue ascent with views to the south.

G **4.9** Reach AT [white-blazed] and turn right (north). Left along AT leads to Bootens Gap parking.

5.3 Climb steadily to Hazeltop Mtn.

B **7.6** Descend gently to intersection with Mill Prong Trail.

A **7.7** Continue on AT and cross drive to Milam Gap Parking.

Hike No. 18

LEWIS FALLS — BLACKROCK

18

Length: 3.3 mi (4.2 mi with spur trails to viewpoints)
Time Estimate: 2 ½ hr (3 hr, incl. spur trails)
Difficulty: Easy
Elev. Change: 1000 ft (1200 ft, incl. spur trails)

Description: Lewis Falls on Hawksbill Creek is one of the highest waterfalls in the park (81 ft). Less than 1 mi from Skyline Drive, it is also one of the most accessible year-round. In winter, water may be flowing beneath ice that sheaths the falls. When not enveloped or swept by clouds, the cliff of Blackrock (3720 ft) has one of the best views in the park. Beyond the Shenandoah River's South Fork, the 50 mi length of Massanutten Mtn can be seen bisecting the valley. Little North Mtn and the Allegheny Mtns rise beyond Massanutten; to the right (north) Stony Man is close and Hawksbill even closer. Just below is the town of Stanley. Jutting into the valley at left is the Shenandoah Salient, a domal upwarp. The distinctive ridges leading out from its center were created by younger, overlying rocks.

Access: The trailhead is a gated service road on the west side of Skyline Drive, 0.5 mi south of MP 51. There are three parking spaces next to the service road (+ one space for handicapped). More spaces (7) are 150 yd north, at the head of Rapidan Road across the Drive. Big Meadows Wayside and the Visitors Center, 0.2 mi north, have ample parking.

Directions:

A   **0.0** Descend service road from Drive; in 100 yd cross narrow horse trail [yellow-blazed] and continue down toward the AT.

B   **0.2** Cross AT [white-blazed]. A few steps below and left is Lewis Spring, the source of Hawksbill Creek.

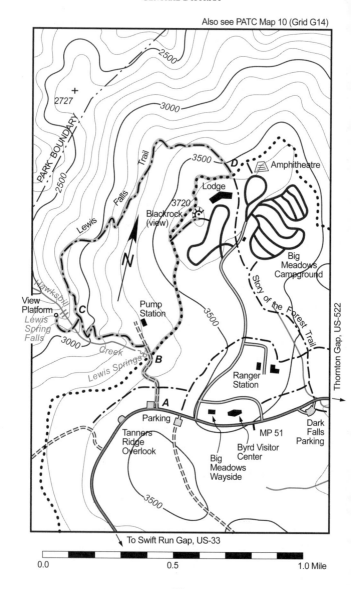

0.0   0.5   1.0 Mile

A padlocked door leads to an underground enclosure for the covered main flow of the spring, which supplies Big Meadows. Water is pumped from this area to the Meadows. A bit further down the service road, turn left at a concrete signpost onto Lewis Falls Trail [blue-blazed].

C   **0.9** At another concrete marker, go 150 yd left on a spur trail [blue-blazed] that crosses the stream above the falls and leads to a stone-walled observation point to view the falls from above. *To continue the hike,* backtrack to Lewis Falls Trail and go left, initially northward along the west

View across Blackrock

ern slope, then follow a sharp bend to the east and climb several hundred ft. In winter much of this stretch of trail offers good views to the west.

D   **2.1** Turn right onto the AT and head back south along the same western slope of the Big Meadows area.

     2.4 Just after passing below Blackrock cliffs, go left at another concrete signpost onto a spur trail [blue-blazed] that leads, in 250 yd, to the top of Blackrock. Then return to AT and continue south.

B   **3.1** Turn left onto service road, leaving the AT to climb back to Skyline Drive.

A   **3.3** Arrive back at trailhead on the Drive.

Hike No. 19

SOUTH RIVER FALLS

19

	Short Circuit	Long Circuit
Length:	4.4 mi	10.2 mi
Time Estimate:	2 hr 45 min	5 hr 45 min
Difficulty:	Easy	Moderate
Elev. Change:	800 ft	1800 ft

Description: Both circuits use South River Falls Trail, a graded trail down South River's deep, wooded gorge to the third-highest waterfall in the Park. The fall's upper and lower cascades drop a total of 83 ft. The Short Circuit takes a quick route to the falls. The Long Circuit first heads north along the AT. It passes Kites Deadening, once the site of farm fields that were cultivated in an unusual way. Rather than felling trees, early settlers including the Kites removed the lower bark, killing them and bringing more sunlight to ground. They planted crops among the dead trees—thus "Kites Deadening." Near the north apex, the route passes Pocosin Cabin, locked but available for use by advance reservation with PATC. "Pocosin" is said to be Native American for "wet" or "swamp." On the return leg, the circuit passes ruins of Upper Pocosin Mission and a cemetery before reaching South River Falls. **Remember "Leave No Trace" ethics (See introduction) and avoid disturbing historic sites along this circuit.**

Access: Go to South River Picnic Area, east off Skyline Drive, 0.2 mi north of MP 63.

Directions for Short Circuit:
A   **0.0** Begin hike at sign for South River Falls Trail [blue-blazed] at eastern (lower) part of loop road through South River Picnic Area.

B   **0.1** Cross AT [white-blazed] and continue downhill on South River Falls Trail.

   1.0 Continue descending to stone-walled viewpoint just beyond the top of falls. (Do not take any spur trails here. Park Service blocks them because this area is dangerous.)

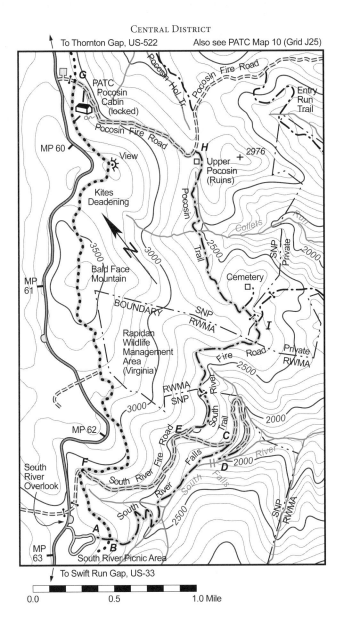

Pocosin Cabin

C **1.2** At concrete post turn right and descend on fire road.

D **1.8** At South River, turn right onto rough foot trail which leads upstream 450 ft to base of falls.

2.0 After retracing steps downstream, reach South River Falls Trail and fire road and begin climbing.

C **2.6** Pass horse hitching post.

E **3.0** Turn left onto South River Fire Road [yellow-blazed] and climb.

F **3.8** Turn left (south) onto AT.

4.3 Turn right onto South River Falls Trail [blue-blazed] at four-way intersection.

A **4.4** Arrive back at South River Falls Picnic Area.

Long Circuit Directions:

A **0.0** Begin hike at sign for South River Falls Trail [blue-blazed] at eastern (lower) part of loop road through South River Picnic Area.

B **0.1** Turn left (north) onto AT [white-blazed].

F **0.6** Cross South River Fire Road [yellow-blazed]. Begin long, gentle ascent of Bald Face Mtn.

1.5 At concrete marker, pass side trail that goes 0.1 mi left to Drive.

1.9 Rocks to left of trail offer views westward over Drive.

2.2 Reach summit of Bald Face Mtn (3600 ft) and begin gentle descent.

2.9 Cross relatively flat area known as Kites Deadening.

3.1 Reach view north to Lewis Mtn, Hazeltop, Jones Mtn, and Fork Mtn (w/ radio tower); descend via switchbacks.

3.4 Continue past spur trail that leads right, downhill, 250 ft to Pocosin Cabin and spring. Descend gently on AT.

G **3.5** Turn right on Pocosin Horse Fire Rd [yellow-blazed].

3.6 Pass Pocosin Cabin, which is on the right side of the road, and descend into the gap.

H **4.4** Turn right at signpost onto Pocosin Trail [yellow-blazed]. A few ft past this turn, ruins of Upper Pocosin Mission are to left of trail.

4.9 Cross Collets Run, the largest stream in the area.

5.6 Pass through abandoned apple orchard to flat, grassy area and angle right to stay on Pocosin HorseTrail. (Spur trail leads 0.1 mi straight ahead to South River cemetery, which is covered by periwinkles in summer.)

I **5.7** Turn right on South River Fire Road [yellow-blazed].

6.0 Unmarked trail enters from right.

6.5 Cross gate at SNP boundary.

E **7.0** Turn left, downhill, at signpost onto fire road.

C **7.4** Continue straight and downhill on fire road passing concrete post for South River Falls Trail on right [blue-blazed].

D **7.9** At South River turn right onto foot trail which leads 450 ft upstream to base of falls.

8.1 After retracing steps downstream, reach South River Falls Trail and begin climbing back up.

C **8.7** Turn left on South River Falls Trail. Fire road continue uphill.

8.8 Pass stone-walled viewpoint at head of falls. (Do not take any spur trails here. Park Service tries to block all of of them because this area is dangerous.)

B **10.1** Cross AT and continue uphill.

A **10.2** Arrive back at South River Falls Picnic Area.

Also see PATC Map 11 (Grid H8)

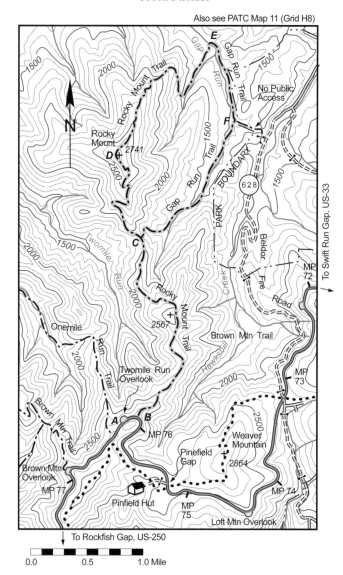

To Rockfish Gap, US-250

0.0	0.5	1.0 Mile

Hike No. 20
ROCKY MOUNT

20

Length:	10.2 mi
Time Estimate:	6 hr 30 min
Difficulty:	Strenuous
Elev. Change:	2600 ft

Description: This circuit traverses a wild, rugged area. The Rocky Mount Trail leads along a side ridge that runs north to the peak of Rocky Mount (2741 ft) with a spectacular view across Twomile Run Valley. Then the trail descends steeply 400 ft on a rough, rocky trail to Gap Run.

Access: Trail begins at sharp curve in Skyline Drive just south of MP 76 and just north of Twomile Run Overlook. Park at the Overlook.

Directions:

A 0.0 From Twomile Run Overlook, walk north along Drive.

B 0.2 At concrete post, go left onto Rocky Mount Trail [blue-blazed] and follow ridge north with many fine views.

C 2.4 In sag, continue on Rocky Mount Trail past Gap Run Trail [blue-blazed], which comes in from right. (Return route comes to this point.) Climb past views of Twomile Run Valley to summit of Rocky Mount.

D 3.6 Cliffs near summit offer fine views. Descend steeply from summit toward Gap Run.
4.7 Begin series of switchbacks as trail gets rocky.
5.2 Cross small stream twice.

E 5.6 Ford Gap Run, then turn right at concrete post onto Gap Run Trail [blue-blazed].

F 6.4 Keep right on Gap Run Trail where old road enters straight ahead.

C 7.8 Turn left at concrete post onto Rocky Mount Trail

B 10.0 Arrive back at Drive. Turn right and walk south along Drive toward Twomile Run Overlook.

A 10.2 Reach overlook parking area.

Hike No. 21

ROCKY MOUNTAIN — BROWN MOUNTAIN

21

Length:	10.1 mi
Time Estimate:	6 hr 30 min
Difficulty:	**Strenuous—recommended for experienced hikers only**
Elev. Change:	2100 ft

Description: The park's South District has a Rocky Mount, a Rocky Mountain, and a Rockytop. The name-givers were obviously impressed with the rugged cliffs, rock slides, and stony streams here. This circuit follows the crest of the Rocky Mountain—Brown Mountain ridge to the summits of Rocky Mtn (2864 ft) and Brown Mtn (2560 ft). This east-west ridge offers extraordinary views: to the north is the lower Twomile Ridge, with Rocky Mount in the background; to the south is the high, imposing ridge that leads to Rockytop. Between the crest of Rocky Mtn and Brown Mtn, fires in 1986 and later years have affected vegetation. The area has a profusion of turkeybeard, a grass-like member of the lily family, and many stands of mountain laurel, all of which bloom in late May-early June. Brown Mountain's sandstone ridge is streaked with 500 million-year-old fossil worm holes, which appear as long, slender cylindrical markings about an eighth of an inch in diameter. Leaving the ridges, the circuit dips into Big Run Valley, then climbs back along Rocky Mountain Run, fording these streams several times. Bring sandals or extra footwear, as the fords may require wading if water is high. Fire and gypsy moths have destroyed many trees in some areas, so shade may be limited. Be sure to carry extra water in summer.

Access: Go to Brown Mtn Overlook on Skyline Drive just north of MP 77 and park.

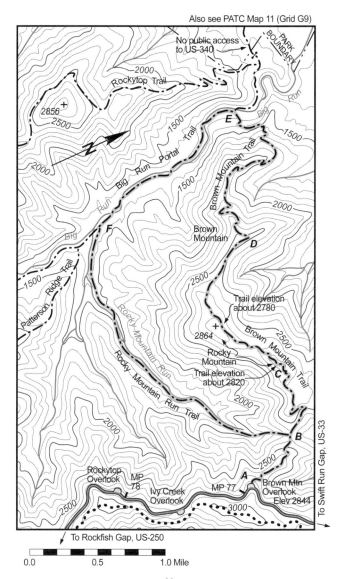

Also see PATC Map 11 (Grid G9)

No public access to US-340

PARK BOUNDARY

2000
Rockytop Trail

2856
2500

Big Run

E

Big Run Portal Trail

1500

1500

2000

Brown Mountain Trail

1500

Big Run

F

2000

Brown Mountain

D

2500

Trail elevation about 2780

2864

Brown Mountain Trail

2500

Rocky Mountain Run Trail

Rocky Mountain Run

Rocky Mountain

Trail elevation about 2820

2500

1500

Patterson Ridge Trail

1500

2000

C

2000

2000

B

Rockytop Overlook

MP 78

Ivy Creek Overlook

MP 77

A

Brown Mtn Overlook Elev 2844

2500

3000

To Swift Run Gap, US-33

To Rockfish Gap, US-250

0.0   0.5   1.0 Mile

Directions:

A **0.0** Go through opening in retaining wall at Brown Mtn Overlook (marked by signpost) and descend on Brown Mtn Trail [blue-blazed].

B **0.7** Reach concrete post at gap where Rocky Mtn Run Trail [blue-blazed] enters on left. (Return route comes to this point.) Continue straight on Brown Mtn Trail.

C **1.6** Other than Brown Mtn Overlook, reach the highest point of the circuit along the crestline of Rocky Mtn, with views west to Massanutten Mtn. Beyond this point, footing becomes rugged as trail descends slightly and then climbs toward second peak.

2.2 Pass to the north side of the highest peak of Rocky Mtn. crest line. Fossil worm holes are visible in outcrops here. Short bushwacks to rock outcrops are rewarded by extraordinary views. Descend slightly and then climb.

D **3.1** Descend from summit of Brown Mtn along ridge crest that offers spectacular views of Shenandoah Valley, Rocky-top, and southern end of Massanutten Mtn. Outcrops on left of trail show fossil worm holes. Turn off ridge line and descend steeply.

E **5.3** Reach Big Run and turn left onto Big Run—Portal Trail [yellow-blazed]. (To right 0.5 mi is "The Portal," a narrow gorge with impressive cliffs and talus slopes.) Continue upstream on trail and ford Big Run twice.

6.3 To left of trail is flat, brushy area that was once a field. Evidence of an old homestead can be seen. Continue on trail, fording the run twice more.

F **6.7** At fork, turn left onto Rocky Mtn Run Trail [blue-blazed] and climb steadily along Rocky Mtn Run, crossing run several times.

B **9.4** Turn right, uphill, at concrete post onto Brown Mtn Trail.

A **10.1** Arrive back at Brown Mtn Overlook.

Hike No. 22
BIG RUN LOOP TRAIL

22

	Short Circuit	*Long Circuit*
Length:	6.0 mi	7.0 mi
Time Estimate:	3 hr 45 min	4 hr 15 min
Difficulty:	Moderate	Moderate
Elev. Change:	1400 ft	1600 ft

Description: Both circuits descend 1140 ft from Big Run Over-look on Skyline Drive to the upper end of Big Run Valley, then climb onto the ridge that defines the Big Run watershed. Here they join the Appalachian Trail and parallel Skyline Drive back to the Overlook. The Long Circuit reaches Browns Gap, which General Stonewall Jackson used to move troops several times during the Civil War's Valley Campaign.

Access: Both circuits begin at Big Run Overlook, just south of MP 81 on Skyline Drive. Parking areas at Big Run Overlook are usually full on summer weekends. Alternate parking is at Doyles River Parking Area, just north of MP 82. (If you park at Doyles River Parking Area, follow AT [white-blazed] north to Doyles River Trail [blue-blazed] to get to point [**A**].)

Directions for Short Circuit:

A **0.0** From Big Run Overlook descend steeply via switch-backs on Big Run Loop Trail [blue-blazed here].
0.7 Trail swings left and descends more gradually.
1.2 Cross rivulet and swing right.

B **2.2** Just below confluence of two small tributaries, cross branch of Big Run. Shortly after, at Big Run—Portal Trail [yellow-blazed], turn left to stay on Big Run Loop Trail [yellow-blazed].Climb steadily through standing dead trees along ravine above branch of Big Run.
3.0 Nearing head of usually dry ravine turn sharply right at switchback and continue ascent up and out of the ravine.

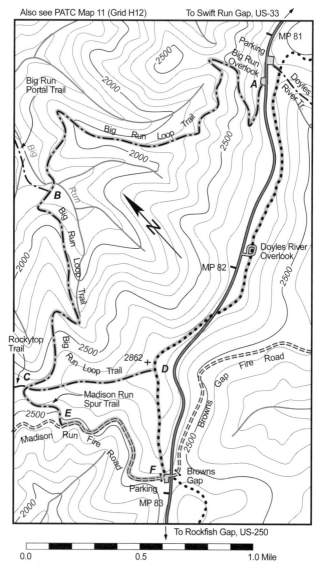

Also see PATC Map 11 (Grid H12)   To Swift Run Gap, US-33

MP 81

Parking
Big Run
Overlook

A

Doyles River Tr.

Big Run
Portal Trail

Big   Run   Loop   Trail

2500

2000

Big

Run

2000

B

Big Run Loop Trail

Doyles River Overlook

MP 82

N

Rockytop Trail

2500

Big   Run   Loop   Trail

2862 +

D

Browns   Gap   Fire   Road

C

Madison Run Spur Trail

E

2500

Madison   Run   Fire   Road

2500

F

Browns Gap

Parking
MP 83

2000

To Rockfish Gap, US-250

0.0   0.5   1.0 Mile

C **3.6** Turn left, uphill, by concrete post at four-way intersection with Rockytop Trail [blue-blazed] and continue
on Big Run Loop Trail [blue-blazed here].

D **4.2** Turn left (north) onto AT [white-blazed].

4.5 Cross Drive and continue on AT. Crossing area offers
fine view of Cedar Mtn and Trayfoot Mtn.

4.7 Follow ledge that offers views in winter.

4.9 Pass through Doyles River Overlook and continue on
AT.

5.9 Turn left, uphill, onto Doyles River Trail [blue-blazed]
to Doyles River Parking and in a few ft cross Drive.

A **6.0** Arrive back at Big Run Overlook.

Directions for Long Circuit:

A-B Follow directions for Short Circuit.

C **3.6** Continue straight across gap onto Madison Run Spur
Trail [yellow-blazed] and descend.

E **3.9** Turn left onto Madison Run Fire Road [yellow-
blazed].

F **4.6** Reach Drive at Browns Gap (2599 ft). Turn left
(north) onto AT [white-blazed] at concrete post in parking lot—Do not cross Drive. Ascend 250 ft and then level
off.

D-A **5.2-7.0** Pass Big Run Loop Trail and continue on AT
across Drive, through Doyles River Overlook, and back
across Drive to Big Run Overlook, following directions
for Short Circuit from 4.2-mile point to the end.

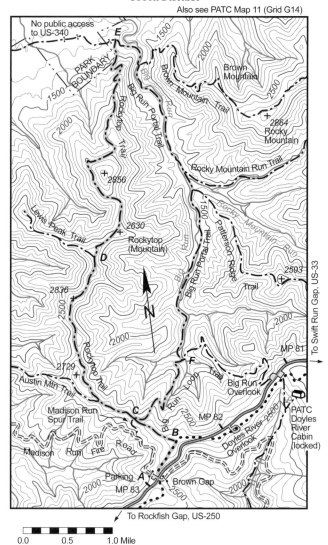

Hike No. 23
BIG RUN/ROCKYTOP

23

Length:	13.8 mi
Time Estimate:	8 hr 30 min
Difficulty:	**Strenuous—recommended for experienced hikers only**
Elev. Change:	2440 ft

Description: This circuit traverses rugged scenery composed of Rockytop's high ridges and deep stream valleys. In all, the route crosses Big Run seven times and side streams twice. These fords become wades when the water is high, as it is much of the year. Sandals or backup footwear is advised. There are spectacular southward views of peaks and the Shenandoah Valley in winter. Summer foliage blocks those views except in the most exposed areas. Rockytop Trail extends across the crest of Rockytop, which forms the sheer southwest wall of Big Run Canyon. Note fossilized worm holes in some of the rock along slides or talus slopes. These long, slender cylindrical markings, about an eighth of an inch in diameter, show that these rocks were once part of a soft seabed. The trail passes many stands of turkeybeard, a grass-like member of the lily family that blooms spectacularly in mid May-early June. Browns Gap, the starting and ending point, was used by Gen. Stonewall Jackson alternately to elude and attack federal forces during the Civil War's Valley Campaign.

Access: Go to Browns Gap Parking Area (2599 ft) on west side of Skyline Drive, 0.1 mi north of MP 83.

Directions:

A   **0.0** Start climbing AT [white-blazed] at concrete post at north edge of parking area.

B   **0.5** Turn left onto Big Run Loop Trail [blue-blazed].

C   **1.2** Reach concrete post at junction with Rockytop Trail [blue-blazed] and Madison Run Spur Trail [yellow-blazed] in hollow. Return route comes to this intersection. Continue straight across hollow onto Rockytop Trail and ascend.

1.6 At fork, go right to continue on Rockytop Trail where Austin Mtn Trail [blue-blazed] enters on left. Skirt right side of ridge, and then swing to left side and cross talus slope that offers views of Austin and Lewis Mtns.

D **3.5** Turn right at intersection with Lewis Peak Trail [blue-blazed] and continue on Rockytop Trail.

4.3 Reach hollow at base of Rockytop's highest peak (2856 ft) and ascend along its western slope.

4.8 Cross talus slope with great views of Austin Mtn and Lewis Mtn to the southwest, and Shenandoah Valley and Massanutten Mtn to north. Many rocks here and on rocky slopes beyond are striated with fossilized worm holes.

5.0 Bear right, ascend by switchbacks over crest of ridge, and then descend. (Hangman Run splits main ridge here.)

E **7.0** Turn right at concrete post onto Big Run—Portal Trail [yellow-blazed]. (A left at the post leads out of park to private road – no public access.) Continue upstream on Big Run—Portal Trail.

7.5 Cross bridge to east bank of Big Run. Pass concrete post and continue on Big Run—Portal Trail where Brown Mtn Trail [blue-blazed] enters on left.

7.9 Make first of several Big Run crossings, all of which may require wading at high water. Cross three more times in the next 0.7 mi.

8.9 Take right fork to stay on Big Run-Portal Trail where Rocky Mtn Run Trail [blue-blazed] enters on left.

9.0 Ford Rocky Mtn Run and cont. on Big Run's east bank.

9.2 Pass concrete post and cont. on Big Run-Portal Trail where Patterson Ridge Trail [yellow-blazed] enters on left.

10.0 Ford Big Run to west bank, cross again in 0.3 mi (good spot for a dip), and yet again 0.1 mi further.

10.5 Cross two small side creeks (last fords)

F **11.4** Turn right at concrete signpost onto Big Run Loop Trail [dual blazed blue and yellow] and begin steady 1.3 mi climb.

C **12.7** At concrete post on ridge, turn left to continue on Big Run Loop Trail [blue-blazed].

B **13.2** Turn right (south) onto AT at concrete post and descend.

A **13.8** Arrive at Browns Gap Parking Area on Drive.

Deer near Raprap Trailhead, South District

Hike No. 24

JONES RUN —
DOYLES RIVER FALLS

24

Circuit:	Short	Medium	Long
Length:	4.7	7.0 mi	8.4 mi
Time Estimate:	3 hr 15 min	4 hr	5 hr
Difficulty:	Easy	Moderate	Moderate
Elev. Change:	900 ft	1400 ft	1800 ft
Map points:	E-F-G-C-D-E	A-B-C-G-A	A-B-C-D-E-F-G-A

Description: These rewarding circuits along the east slope of the Blue Ridge were constructed by the Civilian Conservation Corps (CCC) during the Depression. They visit majestic cascades along Doyles River and Jones Run. The streams have cut deep gorges with broken, precipitous cliffs and enormous, old tulip poplars. Equally grand hemlocks used to rival them, but were killed in the late 1990s, victims of an accidental import, the woolly adelgid insect. The Short Circuit visits the upper falls of Doyles River. The Medium and Long Circuits descend 1330 ft past lovely cascades on Jones Run, and then climb the steep, narrow trail along Doyles River past its lower and upper cascades. All three circuits touch Browns Gap, where the first road was built in 1805 to connect the town of Grottoes in the Valley to Charlottesville on the east side of the Blue Ridge. Named for a settler family on the east slope, Browns Gap Road changes its name to Madison Road, in honor of another settler family on the western slope, as it crosses the Drive. Confederate Gen. Stonewall Jackson used the road to maneuver his troops during the Civil War, often confounding federal forces with his ability to appear and disappear in the rugged terrain. One of Jackson's men was buried just off Browns Gap Road. The Gap road remained popular until closed to the public as the Park opened in 1936.

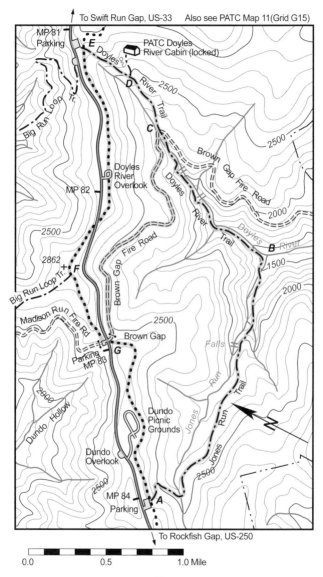

Directions for Short Circuit:

E **0.0** Take Doyles River Trail [blue-blazed] 200 ft to AT [white-blazed]. Turn right (south) onto AT. Trail closely parallels Drive and is fairly level.

0.9 Continue through Doyles River Overlook and follow ledges that offer excellent views south in winter.

1.2 Cross Drive. Cedar and Trayfoot Mtns are visible from this area.

F **1.6** Pass Big Run Loop Trail [blue-blazed], which enters on right. Continue on AT and descend gradually.

G **2.0** Pass concrete post marking Madison Run Fire Road [yellow-blazed] at Browns Gap Parking Area (2599 ft). Continue on AT through parking lot and in 100 ft cross Drive, angling left.

2.1 Turn left onto Browns Gap Fire Road [yellow-blazed] and descend gently.

2.5 On left, a short, steep, rough path leads to a concrete marker at William H. Howard's grave.

3.6 Continue on fire road past ancient tulip poplar of tremendous girth.

C **3.8** Cross metal footbridge and reach intersection with Doyles River Trail.

For side trip to upper falls: Turn right at concrete marker and descend to falls, then return via same trail (0.6 mi round trip).

To continue circuit: Turn left onto Doyles River Trail [blue-blazed] and ascend.

D **4.4** Pass spur trail and spring on right. (Spur trail leads steeply uphill 0.1 mi to Doyles River Cabin, PATC cabin for use by advance reservation only.) Other sources of the Doyle are downhill on left.

E **4.7** 200 ft after crossing AT, arrive at Doyles River Parking Area.

Directions for Medium Circuit:

A **0.0** Descend eastward from Jones Run Parking Area on Jones Run Trail [blue-blazed]. Cross AT [white-blazed] in 100 ft and continue descending.

0.2 Bear right. (Left fork is a utility corridor to Dundo Picnic Grounds; a former CCC camp built in 1937.)

0.6 Cross Jones Run.

1.5 Return to Jones Run and follow south bank.

1.6 Jones Run forms sloping cascade.

1.7 Pass top of 42 ft waterfall. Short spur trail provides good view of falls.

1.8 Reach base of upper falls at concrete post after sharp switchback and big greenstone rock on left.

2.0 Pass top of lower falls. Shortly, enter area with old-growth tulip trees, including a giant with 4.5 ft diameter. Among the trees find diverse flora including walking ferns, bloodroot, wild ginger, white snakeroot, fall wood asters, hepatica and impatiens.

B   **2.4** Just before junction of Jones Run and Doyles River, the trail swings left and crosses Jones Run. Shortly, Jones Run Trail turns into Doyles River Trail at a concrete marker. This area supports a wide variety of wildflowers such as bloodroot, Dutchman's breeches, cutleaf toothwort, and hepatica. Continue circuit on Doyles River Trail [blue-blazed], climbing alongside Doyles River.

3.1 Reach concrete post marking base of lower falls.

3.4 Reach upper falls.

3.7 Cross Doyles River

C   **3.8** Turn left onto Browns Gap Fire Road [yellow-blazed] and climb through another ancient tulip poplar grove.

5.1 To right, short footpath leads to concrete grave marker for William H. Howard, Company F, 44th VA Infantry, CSA.

G   **5.4** Turn left (south) on AT [white-blazed] at Browns Gap (Do not cross Drive to parking lot) and begin climb.

6.2 Reach concrete marker for Dundo Picnic Grounds, where water can be obtained from May to October. Continue on AT, passing Dundo side trails

A   **7.0** Arrive back at Jones Run Parking Area.

Directions for Long Circuit:

A-B Follow directions for Medium Circuit.

C   **3.8** Cross Browns Gap Fire Road [yellow-blazed] and continue climbing on Doyles River Trail.

D   **4.4** Pass stonewalled spring on right of trail. (Spur trail leads right 0.1 mi steeply uphill to Doyles River Cabin, PATC cabin for use by advance reservation only.)

E   **4.6** Turn left (south) onto AT. Trail closely parallels Drive and is fairly level.

  5.5 Follow AT through Doyles River Overlook.

  5.9 Cross Drive. Cedar Mtn is visible to the east, and Trayfoot Mtn is to the west.

F   **6.2** Stay on AT where Big Run Loop Trail [blue-blazed] enters on right. Begin gradual descent.

G   **6.8** After passing concrete post at Madison Fire Rd in Browns Gap Parking Area (2599 ft) and turning left to reach Skyline Drive, cross Drive and angle right, still on AT. (Browns Gap Fire Road descends the eastern slope to the left.)

  7.6 Reach concrete marker for Dundo Picnic Grounds, where water can be obtained from May to October. Continue on AT, passing Dundo's side trails.

A   **8.4** Arrive back at Jones Run Parking Area.

Doyles River Cabin in Autumn

Hike No. 25

AUSTIN MOUNTAIN — FURNACE MOUNTAIN

25

Length:	12.1 mi (13.1 mi with recommended side trip to Furnace Peak)
Time Estimate:	7 hr 45 min (8 hr 15 min w/ side trip)
Difficulty:	**Strenuous—recommended for experienced hikers only**
Elev. Change:	2500 ft (2750 ft with side trip)

Description: This difficult hike ranges west from Browns Gap (2500 ft) to Austin Mtn (2657 ft), dips into the Madison Run drainage (crossing at the 1500 ft elevation point), climbs back onto Furnace Mtn (2658 ft), and returns along ridgelines to Blackrock (3092 ft) and Skyline Drive. The AT at Blackrock Summit offers spectacular views of Trayfoot Furnace Austin Mountains, as well as Madison Run and the Shenandoah Valley beyond. Outlying Austin and Furnace peaks are in one of the Park's most remote wilderness areas. Heavy-duty footwear is recommended, along with an extra measure of caution. Parts of the circuit may be overgrown, and there are several stretches on talus slopes of loose, treacherous rock. Others are steep and poorly graded. Since a poaching ring was broken up, black bear sightings are more frequent. The characteristic black-splatter droppings in the middle of the trail warn that you are on their turf. The 0.5 mi side trail to the summit of Furnace Mtn offers excellent views over the Madison and your entire route. Vultures fly by at eye level between the peaks, seeking hikers and other creatures that have stopped moving.

Access from Skyline Drive: Go to Browns Gap Parking Area, 0.1 mi north of MP 83. Begin circuit at [**A**].

Directions:
A **0.0** Follow the AT North [white-blazed] from concrete

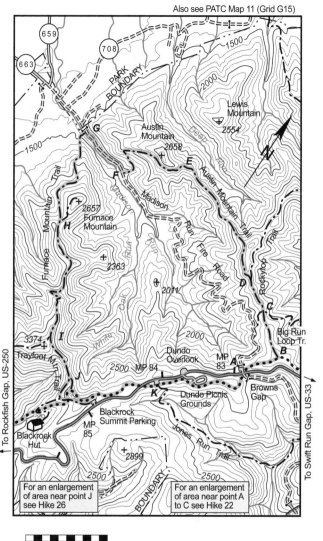

For an enlargement of area near point J see Hike 26

For an enlargement of area near point A to C see Hike 22

0.0   0.5   1.0 Miles

post marking intersection with Madison Run Fire Road [yellow-blazed] on north side of Browns Gap Parking Area (2599 ft). Ascend 250 ft and then level off.

B **0.5** Turn left at concrete post onto Big Run Loop Trail [blue-blazed].

C **1.2** Concrete post marks junction with Rockytop Trail [blue-blazed] and Madison Run Spur Trail [yellow-blazed]. Continue straight ahead onto Rockytop Trail and ascend.

D **1.6** Fork left to begin long descent on Austin Mtn Trail [blue-blazed].

E **3.4** Trail dips and veers left.

3.7 Descend steeply across rock slopes below cliffs. Views of Madison Run, Shenandoah Valley.

4.3 Hairpin turn left around stump, still descending.

4.6 Begin following seasonal streambed in area with a flattened circle – perhaps where settlers made charcoal.

F **4.8** Turn right onto Madison Run Fire Road [yellow-blazed].

G **5.4** Turn left at concrete post onto Furnace Mtn Trail [blue-blazed]. Cross Madison Run and follow it downstream for about 100 ft before beginning to climb Furnace Mtn. (In summer, trail along run may be obscured by new growth.)

H **7.0** Spur trail [blue-blazed] enters on left.

To go to peak of Furnace Mtn: Turn left onto spur trail and hike 0.5 mi to ledge with excellent view of Madison Run Valley, Austin Mtn across the valley and Blue Ridge on right.

To continue circuit: Continue uphill on Furnace Mtn Trail from junction with spur trail at **[H]**.

8.1 Turn sharply left to stay on Furnace Mtn Trail.

I **8.7** Turn left onto Trayfoot Mtn Trail [blue-blazed].

J **9.3** Turn left onto Blackrock Spur Trail [blue-blazed] at concrete post in frequently overgrown area and enter area with striking rock formations.

9.5 At end of spur trail, turn left (north) onto AT [white-blazed]. Continue along AT at Blackrock Summit with spectacular views to the west.

9.8 AT and Trayfoot Mtn Trail come within a few ft of one another and run parallel for about 0.1 mi, but do not cross.

9.9 At concrete post, AT is briefly concurrent with blue-blazed Trayfoot Mtn Trail, which leads right 750 ft to Drive and parking lot. Continue on AT.

10.6 Cross to east side of Drive and pass through remains of abandoned apple orchard.

K **10.8** Pass Jones Run Trail [blue-blazed]. (Parking lot is 50 ft to left.) Continue on AT along fairly level terrain.

11.4 Continue straight on AT where spur trail leads left to Dundo Picnic Grounds. (Water is available at Dundo from May to October.) Descend gradually.

A **12.1** Cross Skyline Drive to parking area at end of fire road.

Hike No. 26
BLACKROCK

26

Length: 1.7 mi
Time Estimate: 1 hr
Difficulty: Easy
Elev. Change: 330 ft

Description: This short circuit offers an excellent experience in one of the Park's wilderness areas, on a variety of trails. Blackrock (3092 ft) is a tumbled mass of lichen-covered boulders that offers spectacular views. [C]. Like other rocky slopes in this part of the park, Blackrock was once a huge cliff. Long ago the cliff crumbled and tumbled down the mountainside. The uneven surfaces that can be seen in the rocks were once cliff tops. Smooth surfaces indicate where the rocks split.

Access: Park in paved Blackrock Summit Parking area on west side of Skyline Drive approxi¬mately 0.6 mi south of MP 84.

Directions:
A **0.0** Walk past map poster and around yellow-painted gate on south side of parking lot and begin with a brief climb up Trayfoot Mtn Trail [blue-blazed].
B **0.1** At concrete post, AT and Trayfoot Mtn Trail touch. Angle right onto AT [white-blazed]. Continue uphill (south) as AT parallels Trayfoot Mtn Trail.
C **0.5** Turn right onto Blackrock Spur Trail [blue-blazed] at concrete post amid interesting jumble of boulders. After passing through cleft rock formation, trail ahead enters wooded area.
D **0.7** At concrete marker, turn sharply left, almost doubling back, onto Trayfoot Mtn Trail [blue-blazed] and pass excellent views.
E **1.0** Turn left onto Blackrock Hut Fire Road to stay on Trayfoot Mtn Trail.

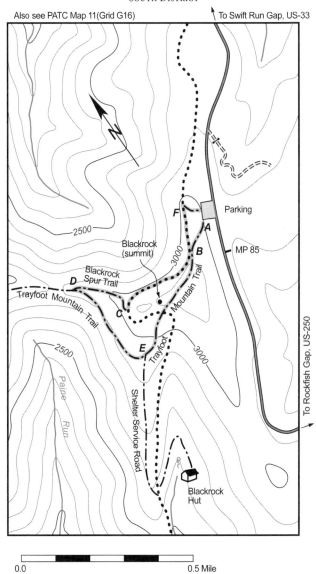

1.2 Cross AT near top of ridge and continue up service road. Shortly after, pass over top of ridge. Trees and brush here screen the barren rockpile out of sight a short distance to the left.

B **1.5** At concrete post where AT and Trayfoot Mtn Trail touch, angle left onto AT and continue downhill (north).

F **1.7** Turn right onto short connector trail and arrive back at parking area on Drive.

Blackrock with Measuring Wheel

Hike No. 27

TRAYFOOT MOUNTAIN— PAINE RUN

27

Length:	9.6 mi
Time Estimate:	6 hr
Difficulty:	Strenuous
Elev. Change:	2200 ft

Description: This hike begins at Blackrock Gap (2329 ft) and climbs on the Appalachian Trail to Blackrock (3092 ft), a tumbled mass of lichen-covered stone that offers spectacular year-round views. Then the hike climbs Trayfoot Mountain on a trail that follows an old fire road. After reaching Trayfoot's summit (3374 ft), it descends along a ridge that offers many fine views to Paine Run, then climbs back along Paine Run to Blackrock Gap. This climb passes Buzzard Rock, a sharp peak, and the site of the former Blackrock Springs Hotel.

Access: Park at Blackrock Gap (NOT the Blackrock Summit lot further north) between MP 87 and MP 88 on west side of Skyline Drive, roughly halfway between northern (Swift Run Gap) and southern (Rockfish Gap) access points for the South District of the Park.

Directions:

A   **0.0** Cross to east side of Drive and turn left (north) onto AT [white-blazed].
   0.2 Cross Drive again and stay on AT. Ahead is gradual climb (0.2 mi), then a fork where AT angles slightly to left.
   0.7 Stay on AT as it intersects blue-blazed trail. Right leads steeply downhill 0.2 mi to Blackrock Hut (for long-distance AT hikers only) and its nearby spring in deep ravine. To left is hut service road, which shortly swings parallel to AT. Begin long climb along eastern side of ridge on AT.

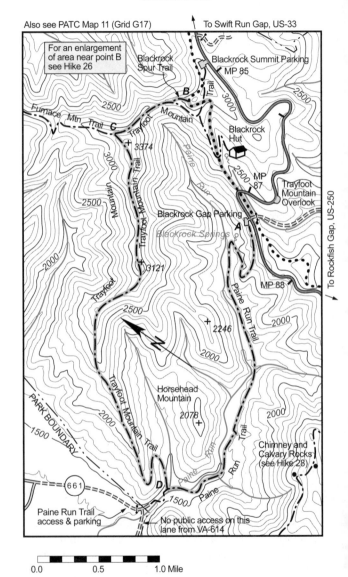

1.2 Cross Trayfoot Mtn Trail [blue-blazed], which leads to Blackrock Summit Parking Area 0.6 mi on right, and continue on AT. In 300 ft, begin to circle Blackrock. This section of trail offers great year-round views over boulder-strewn slope.

B **1.3** Turn left at concrete marker onto Blackrock Spur Trail [blue-blazed] and descend through maze of rock.

1.5 At next concrete post, bear right onto Trayfoot Mtn Trail [blue-blazed] and shortly begin ascent of Trayfoot Mtn.

C **2.0** Pass Furnace Mtn Trail [blue-blazed], which enters on right, and continue left to climb ridge on Trayfoot Mtn Trail.

2.2 Reach summit of Trayfoot Mtn. (Old road leads left to site of fire tower.) Begin gradual 3.2 mi descent with occasional rises over knobs. Both sides of trail offer views.

5.4 Rocky ledge offers excellent view of Buzzard Rock across Paine Run. From here, trail veers left to start a series of long switchbacks down to Paine Run.

D **6.0** Just before streambed of a Paine Run tributary, trail swings right to parallel the stream. In 50 ft, turn left to onto Paine Run Trail [yellow-blazed] on old fire road at concrete post and cross the intermittent tributary.

6.3 After a fairly easy stretch with Paine Run on right, cross it (may be high after rain) and begin long climb. Next 1.5 mi brings 5 stream crossings, most on intermittent tributaries.

8.5 Cross 2 intermittent feeder creeks about 100 ft apart.

8.7 Continue climbing steeply in old road bed.

A **9.6** Arrive back at Blackrock Gap Parking Area.

Hike No. 28
RIPRAP HOLLOW

28

Length:	9.5 mi
Time Estimate:	5 hr 45 min
Difficulty:	Moderate
Elev. Change:	2300 ft

Description: This beautiful circuit passes through an interesting area of ecological succession that still shows signs of three fires in 1990s. The route passes excellent views at Calvary Rocks and Chimney Rocks and descends along Meadow Run through Cold Spring Hollow and Riprap Hollow. "Riprap" is the descriptive term for the broken rocks that are abundant in these hollows. The hollows also contain Catawba rhododendron, a common species further south but rare in the park, as well as mountain laurel, fly poison, turkeybeard, starflower, and wild bleeding heart -- All of which bloom in late May. Meadow Run has nice cascades and an excellent swimming hole. The circuit climbs back via the Wildcat Ridge Trail. This circuit can be hiked from either the Wildcat Ridge Parking area or the Riprap Parking Area. Directions are provided from the Riprap Parking Area.

Access from Riprap Parking Area: Park at Riprap Parking Area, a few ft north of MP 90 on west side of Skyline Drive.

Access from Wildcat Parking Area: Park at Wildcat Ridge Parking Area, just south of MP 92 on west side of Drive. Begin circuit at [**E**] on trail map. Hike 0.1 mi down Wildcat Ridge Trail [blue-blazed], turn right (north) onto AT, and follow circuit directions from [**D**].

Directions:

A   0.0 From Riprap Parking Area, take 100 ft spur to AT [white-blazed]. Go right (north) on AT and climb.

B   0.4 At top of knob (2988 ft), go left at concrete post onto

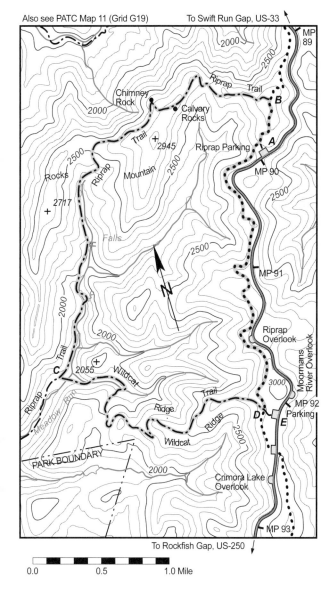

Also see PATC Map 11 (Grid G19)

To Swift Run Gap, US-33

MP 89

Riprap Trail

Chimney Rock

Calvary Rocks

B

A

Riprap Parking

MP 90

Trail

2945

2000

2500

Rocks

Riprap

Mountain

2717

Falls

2500

N

2500

MP 91

Riprap Overlook

Moormans River Overlook

Trail

3000

MP 92

2000

Riprap

Trail

2055

Wildcat

C

Meadow Run

Ridge

Trail

Ridge

D

E

Parking

Wildcat

PARK BOUNDARY

2500

2000

Crimora Lake Overlook

MP 93

To Rockfish Gap, US-250

| 0.0 | 0.5 | 1.0 Mile |

Riprap Trail [blue-blazed]. Begin long, easy descent.

1.4 After a 0.1 mi ascent around and among Calvary Rocks, trail hooks left onto knob. Spur trail on right leads 15 ft to cliffs with excellent vistas.

1.6 After passing more stark rock formations, turn left where spur trail on right leads 75 ft to broken cliffs of Chimney Rock, which offer excellent views north and west.

2.2 Trail turns sharply left, descends steeply at first.

2.9 After grade eases as trail begins following bed of an intermittent stream, the stream's flow becomes regular.

3.3 Past remains of a dam, followed by picturesque cascades, take right fork at sign, climbing up and away from stream. Nice ferns cluster here.

3.5 Cross to east side of Meadow Run.

3.6 Pass deep pool at base of gentle waterfall (excellent swimming hole) amid pink-blooming Catawba rhododendron, and then recross Meadow Run.

C **4.2** Turn left at concrete post onto Wildcat Ridge Trail [blue-blazed], cross Meadow Run, then go left and climb along small stream.

4.4 Cross run and climb to left, then follow sharp right up a switchback. (Unmarked trail at switchback goes back downstream to rock shelter.)

4.7 Recross run and begin long ascent.

5.5 Switchback to left puts trail briefly on north heading, with fine views to southwest.

5.8 Trail levels near knob's summit (2514 ft).

D **6.8** Turn left (north) onto AT and stroll through mountain laurel and a few Catawba rhododendron on west slope, with mostly gentle grade and good tread to the end. (Wildcat Parking Area is 0.1 mi straight ahead at this turn.)

A **9.5** Turn right on spur trail to Riprap Parking Area.

Chimney Rock

Hike No. 29

TURK BRANCH —
MOORMANS RIVER

29

Length: 8.0 mi (or 10.0 mi with side trip)
Time Estimate: 5 hr (or 6 hr 15 min with side trip)
Difficulty: Moderate
Elev. Change: 2030 ft (or 2730 ft with side trip)

Description: This circuit starts at Jarman Gap, follows the Appalachian Trail north to Turk Gap, and then crosses Skyline Drive and descends to the South Fork of Moormans River. Then the circuit returns via South Fork Moormans River Road, which follows the original route of the Appalachian Trail to Jarman Gap. This circuit can be lengthened by taking a strongly recommended side trip (2 mi round trip) to the summit of Turk Mountain (2981 ft), which offers outstanding views. The rock on the summit is a type of sandstone full of fossil worm holes, which give the rock a striated appearance. From mid-May into early June, turkeybeard, a member of the lily family, blooms along the trail.

Access: Park at Jarman Gap, which is 0.3 mi north of MP 97 on east side of Skyline Drive.

Directions:
A **A 0.0** From left (north) side of entrance to Jarman Gap parking, descend past barrier chain across Moormans River Road [yellow-blazed].
  0.1 Turn left (north) onto AT [white-blazed] and descend along west bank of Moormans River, which is just small creek here. Then leave creek and climb hill.
  0.7 Partway up hill, cross grass-covered pipeline.
  1.2 Reach hill's summit. Bucks Elbow Mtn is visible to rear (east). Descend past views west to Turk Mtn, Sawmill Ridge, and outskirts of Waynesboro.

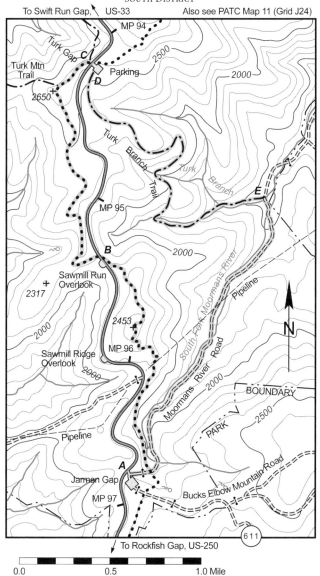

B **1.8** Cross Drive and begin climbing.

3.2 Reach summit of knob (2650 ft) and continue on AT. Turk Mtn Trail [blue-blazed] enters on left in 100 yd.

To take side trip to Turk Mtn: Turn left onto Turk Mtn Trail, continue to summit, and then return via same trail (2.0 mi round trip).

To continue circuit: Continue north on AT.

C **3.5** Cross Drive at concrete post for Turk Gap (2625 ft). At parking lot entrance across Drive, turn right onto Turk Branch Trail [yellow-blazed] and head south, parallel to Drive.

D **3.8** Follow Turk Branch Trail left, away from Drive, and begin descent on eroded section in area of dying pines. Moccasin flowers put on an excellent show here in spring.

4.8 Cross stream. Trail improves as continues descent in hardwood forest. Cross stream three more times.

E **6.0** Turn right onto South Fork Moormans River Road [yellow-blazed] and follow it.

7.9 Cross AT and continue on South Fork Moormans River Road.

A **8.0** Arrive back at parking area at Jarman Gap.

PATC Guidebooks

The following guides are available from the Potomac Appalachian Trail Club (PATC). In addition, the PATC publishes books of historical and general interest. To learn more, or to place an order, visit the PATC website, www.patc.net or contact PATC at 703 242-0315.

Guidebooks:

- *AT Guide to Shenandoah National Park and Side Trails*
- *AT Guide Set to Shenandoah (includes AT Guide to Shenandoah with all maps to the park)*
- *AT Guide to Maryland and Northern Virginia*
- *AT Guide Set to Maryland (includes AT Guide to Maryland and Northern Virginia, AT Maryland map and both AT Northern Virginia maps)*
- *Guide to Massanutten Mountain*
- *Massanutten Guide Set (Guide to Massanutten Mountain with Massanutten maps to North and South Half*
- *Circuit Hikes in Shenandoah National Park*
- *Circuit Hikes in Virginia, West Virginia, Maryland and Pennsylvania*
- *Hikes in Western Maryland*
- *The Tuscarora Trail North (Guide to MD and PA)*
- *The Tuscarora Trail South (Guide to WV and VA)*
- *Hikes in Washington: Part A Northern Maryland Counties*
- *Hikes in Washington: Part B Northern Virginia Counties*
- *Hikes in Washington: Part C DC/Southern Maryland Counties*
- *Guide to Great North Mountain Trails*
- *Climbers Guide to the Great Falls of the Potomac*
- *Carderock Past & Present: A Climber's Guide*

NOTES